# HOW TO WRITE

Stephen Leacock

# How To Write

JUNIOR NOVITIATE

Dodd, Mead & Company
New York          1943

PRINTED IN THE UNITED STATES OF AMERICA
AMERICAN BOOK—STRATFORD PRESS, INC., NEW YORK

# PREFACE

In writing this book I have endeavoured to avoid as far as possible all reference to authors and books of the immediate hour. Still more have I avoided anything like criticism of them. The reason for this is obvious enough. The purpose of the book is to help people to write and not to offer criticism of authors' attempts to do so. Our language has come down to us with so little change since the days of Shakespeare that we have a field of three and a half centuries from which to select examples of style, illustrations of method, and fields for analysis. It is only in a few aspects, such as in slang and in swearing, that our language of today needs discussion by itself.

A further reason for avoiding citation of living authors is found in the growing difficulties which surround literary quotation today. In these complicated days of movie and radio production copyrights are so jealously guarded that not even a fragment must be borrowed. There is no longer the free and careless quotation that was once as open to all as was the old-time apple orchard to the passer-by. One can only borrow with impunity now from those whose rest can no longer be broken by it.

This book is in part the outcome of personal experience and personal sympathy. I did not personally get started writing, except for a few odd pieces, until I was forty years old. Like the milkmaid with a fortune in her face I had a fortune (at least as good as hers) in my head. Yet I spent ten weary years as an impecunious schoolmaster without ever realizing this asset. The fault, like that of Abdul the Bulbul Ameer, was "entirely my own." I had too little courage, was too sensitive. I had a little initial success with odd humorous writings in the earlier nineties. I can see now that the proportion of success I had was exceptionally high and that the rejection of a manuscript should have meant no more than the blow of a feather. Still more did I fail in not knowing where to find material for literary work. It seemed to me that my life as a resident schoolmaster was so limited and uninteresting that there was nothing in it to write about. Later on, when I had learned how, I was able to turn back to it and write it up with great pecuniary satisfaction. But that was after I had learned how to let nothing get past me. I can write up anything now at a hundred yards.

So, for this and that reason, my efforts towards humorous writing died away and I lived on in my forsaken garden. Years later I left school teaching, took up graduate study and became a lecturer in Political Science at McGill University. As years went by I decided that if the garden of fancy was not for me, I could at least work underground. So I took my pick and shovel to the college library and in three years I completed my *Elements of Political Science*. This book had an outstanding, indeed an ominous, success. It was no sooner adopted as the text book by the renovated government of China, than the anti-Manchu rebellion swept the former Empire. The Khedive of Egypt's attempt to use it as the text book of the Egyptian schools, was followed by the nationalist outbreak.

But for me the writing of it had a peculiar effect. I found that again and again I wanted to put something funny into it. I was sure I could describe much better the nature of British government if I were allowed to put in a dialogue between the Keeper of the Swans and the Clerk of the Cheque, or the Master of the Bloodhounds. I refer, of course, to all those queer officials in England who sound like a winning hand at poker. In them really lies the essence of British government, British character and British success.

So when the *Political Science* was done I tried again. I gathered up the bygone manuscripts and wrote some new ones and sent them out as *Literary Lapses*. After that it was all easy. I was like Artemus Ward's weary prisoner, behind his locked door, who opened the window and got out. But meantime I was forty years old.

I say all this not for the pleasure of writing about myself, although that is considerable, but in the hope that it may be of use to other younger people. No matter how restricted your life is (I am speaking to them now personally), there is plenty of material in it and around you to write about. Your father, for instance, couldn't you do something with him? . . . or, if not your father, then, at any rate, Uncle Joe, because everybody says he's a regular character. . . .

And with that I put the book into your hands with my best wishes.

STEPHEN LEACOCK

McGill University
Montreal
October 1942

# CONTENTS

# CHAPTER 1

## THE DESIRE TO WRITE

*Writing means thinking — Consider, William, take a month to think — The desire to write a natural impulse like wanting to be a policeman — Inspiration versus effort — This came to me, says the poet — Learning to see and learning to say what you see — Unwritten masterpieces of non-starters*

THE bygone humorist Bill Nye once inserted in his column of Answers to Correspondents an enthusiastic item which read, "You write a splendid hand, you ought to write for the papers." The wilful confusion of mind as to what writing means is very funny. But the confusion is no hazier than that of many young people who "want to write." Bill Nye would have told them that the best writing is done straight from the elbow. It is the purpose of this book to show that it originates in the brain. Writing is thinking.

This confusion between writing as a form of activity and as a form of thought came down to us from the long years during which the mechanical art of writing seemed of itself scholarship. In our immediate day, very brief in comparison, the art of writing has become practically universal among the nations called civilized. If that were all that were needed, everyone might be an author. Indeed, it is hard for us now to realize how very few people in past ages knew how to write. Charlemagne (742-814), who founded schools of learning in his great Empire, couldn't read or write. He tried to learn but he never succeeded. He used to carry round with him—so wrote a monk who was his friend and biographer—tablets and pencils in the hope that he might find time and opportunity to learn. But it was beyond him. It seems strange to imagine his great frame (he was nearly eight feet high) bent over his copy book as he breathed hard in his stubborn effort. It was his own inability to read that led him to found schools for others. There is something pathetic in this ambition of the greatest towards a thing now possessed by the humblest. It has the same human quality in it as when with us a millionaire, debarred from education in his own youth, founds a university and whenever he learns of something new that he doesn't know, founds a new chair in it.

This general inability to read and write lasted for centuries after Charlemagne. Henry the First of England was called Beau-Clerc, the "fine scholar," presumably merely because he could read and write in Latin: he had no further title to scholarship except that he started the first menagerie: but a little went a long way in those days. The barons of the Magna Carta signed with their seals, not their signatures. They couldn't read it. Even in the England of Queen Victoria's early reign over sixty per cent of the young women of the working class who got married signed the marriage register with their mark. For years after that in the country parts of England a "scholar" meant a person who could read and write as opposed to the generality who couldn't.

It is worth while to make this reference to the ability to write, to the mechanical art of writing and its relative rarity in bygone times, and indeed till yesterday. For to this fact is partly due the rather distorted view frequently taken as to what writing means. It is still thought of as if it meant stringing words together, whereas in reality the main part of it is "thinking." People don't realize this. A student says "I want to write"; he never says "I want to think." Indeed, nobody deliberately wants to think except the heroine in a problem play, who frequently gasps out "I must *think*," a view fully endorsed by the spectators. "Let me *think!*" she says; indeed she probably has to go away, to the Riviera, "to think." When she comes back we learn that she is now looking for some way to "stop thinking"——to prevent her from going mad.

Here and there perhaps are a few other cases of the desire to think. There is a famous statue by Rodin, a statue of a primitive man—with a massive jaw and narrow forehead—seated with his head in his hands, his gaze fixed, his face rigid with an effort towards something still beyond his primitive powers. Yet in his fixed gaze is the hope of the centuries. Rodin called his figure "The Thinker." Yet he might equally well have called him "The Writer," or even "The Editor" —or no, perhaps not the Editor; he's different.

Take another random illustration. We find in Tennyson's works a poem dealing with the rural England of his day in which a farmer, in urging a marriage on his son, says, "Consider, William; take a month to think." Tennyson's accurate knowledge of the English countryside has been much admired. He probably timed this to a day. The advice would have been equally appropriate if William had been wanting to write.

. . . . . . .

All these references are made in order to stress the simple fact that writing is essentially *thinking,* or at least involves thinking as its first requisite. All people can think, or at least they think they think. But few people can say what they think, that is, say it with sufficient power of language to convey it to the full. Even when they have conveyed it, it may turn out to be not worth conveying. But there are some people whose thoughts are so interesting that other people are glad to hear them, or to read them. Yet even these people must learn the use of language adequate to convey their thoughts; people may sputter and gurgle in a highly interesting way but without the full equipment of acquired language their sputters won't carry far. This, then, is what is meant by writing—to have thoughts which are of interest to other people and to put them into language which reveals the thoughts. These thoughts may come in part from native originality, in part from deliberate search and reflection. In all that concerns writing, spontaneous originality, what we call native gift, is mingled with the result of conscious effort. The threads are interwoven in the cloth, till they blend and often seem indistinguishable.

It is the affectation of many authors to lay stress on the spontaneity of their thought. "This came to me," says such a one, striking a pose, "came to me one day in the heart of the woods." Poets have always loved to compare themselves to birds, singing untaught and unrewarded. Orators persuade themselves that they speak best on the spur of the moment. The truth is otherwise. The bird spends its life in practise; the orator has agonized at home.

Now and again indeed the sheer reach of genius may attain a sudden vision beyond precise calculation. Thus Charles Dickens in recording the origin of his most immortal creation said with a sublime simplicity, "Then I thought of Mr. Pickwick." But this is only the case where the simplicity of genius matches the affectation of pretense. It is hard to see how anyone could have *thought* out Mr. Pickwick, gaiter by gaiter and spectacle by spectacle. He had to *come,* with an illumination as sudden as flashlight; but behind the most instantaneous flashlight is an intricate chemical preparation.

It is proper to lay stress on this for those who wish to write. They are apt to be fascinated with what seems to be spontaneous. They like to think of "dashing things off," of ideas coming "like a flash." They read how Rouget de L'Isle composed the *Marseillaise* at one sitting, words, music and all, the sitting being held on a stool in front of a little spinet in an upstairs room in Strasburg in April, 1792. They read how Beckford wrote *Vathek* all at one sitting; how Bret Harte, so Mark Twain said, wrote his marvellously successful story, *Thankful Blossom,* all in one single upstairs session in Mark Twain's house—interrupting it only with calls for more whiskey.

Another legend promoted by the egotism of a certain class of authors represents writing as a process involving infinite groaning and yearning, the writer feeding his readers on his blood, as the flamingo feeds its young. A well-known novelist of today is on record as saying, "There is only one recipe for writing that I ever heard of: take a quart or more of life-blood; mix it with a bottle of ink and a teaspoonful of human tears; and ask God to forgive the blots." It may be a recipe. But a good many writers find it easier to take a quart of whiskey and a teaspoonful of vermouth. Indeed there is no more need to use up life-blood and tears in writing than there is in the real estate business or in dry duck-farming. The Roman poet said that there are tears for everything, but writing is not especially wet.

Such legends multiply and colour the thought of the aspirant; all that is needed, it seems, is to be original enough and quick enough and drunk enough—and you can write anything. Beside this, plodding industry and deliberate effort seem dull stuff. In fact the notion that a thing has been produced by hard work seems to cheapen it. Take this queer illustration. All of us from our earliest childhood recall the song *Way down upon the Swanee River,* and have felt the peculiar yearning to get to the Swanee River and stay there. Yet when the song was written there wasn't any Swanee River in it as its composer, Stephen Foster, had never heard of the Swanee River. "I want," he said to his friends, "to get hold of the name of a river with two syllables that will fit into the words 'way down upon the something-river.'" So they dug up the Swanee off a map. The knowledge of this seems to take some of the wistful yearning out of the song. It's as if the composer of *John Brown's Body Lies a'mouldering in the Grave* had got a grave and got a body and only needed John Brown.

· • • • • • •

What has been written down is not wandering from the point. It is the point itself. It is the main focus of attention, the very center of inquiry:—To what extent and in what way are effortless inspiration and uninspired effort to be combined by people animated by a desire to write?

Now this desire to write on the part of a young person thinking of a career is altogether to be commended. It corresponds with a lot of other natural impulses such as the desire to go fishing, or to hunt something, or to "make" something, to the native human impulse towards creative effort as opposed to the acquired human submissiveness, a thing of yesterday, to a forced activity, carried on for gain and by necessity and not for its own sake. This is what we commonly call "work" and is so defined by the economists. What we call "creative work" ought not to be called work at all, because it isn't.

It is to be noted that the willingness to submit to "work," in the true sense, is an acquired capacity which the human race has taken on, with vast advantage to the mass, within the last ten thousand years or so. Some of us have not got it yet. The Portuguese East Africans have not caught on to it. Our Red Indians would have blushed at it, and even in the higher communities, a certain number of individuals—"tramps," "hoboes," "loafers"—still don't see it. But the rest of us, along with the horse, the ox, the jackass and the elephant are long since broken into "work," to the idea of submitting to the imposition of labour by the hour, often very meaningless in itself, as a condition of living, a sort of compromise between freedom and slavery.

Now every child that is born into the world comes to it with a basis of mentality, an interpretation of life that was fashioned so slowly and so long ago that our ten thousand years of work has nothing to do with it. The child's economic world is a wonderful place, in which everybody is doing things because he wants to do them. The child understands that the furnaceman stokes up the furnace for the glorious fun of making the red glow when the poker hits the coals. So the child decides to be a furnaceman when he grows up. The child sees the policeman on the corner—helmet, baton and buttons, and all authority—directing the traffic, and decides to be a traffic policeman when he grows up. Indeed, he can't wait. In a toy helmet with a toy baton he directs traffic in the nursery, blowing his whistle, and thinking—"Here's the life." Or the child wants to run a streetcar, or to be an elevator man. All his little invented games of play are adaptations and anticipations of "work." But he doesn't know it: the future is veiled.

Gradually the veil is drawn aside. The child begins to understand that the furnaceman is not stoking the fire for fun, that the garbage man doesn't love garbage, and that the streetcar conductor doesn't keep the money, as he does in the nursery. The poet Wordsworth has told how "the shades of the prison house begin to close about the growing boy." He is referring to the boy's soul, gradually bruised into forgetfulness of its own immortal origin. But he might have told it also, with perhaps greater immediate pathos, in the economic sense—the fading of the bright vista of the nursery economic world, and the conversion of its glorious company into people working for money to buy food and clothes.

This conversion, though the child cannot know it, is never in reality quite complete. The human mind has a marvellous quality of adaptation. Many people, blessed with good health and conscience, grow to "like their job," begin to do it as if they did it for its own sake. The janitor of the apartment building becomes in his fancy its proprietor. The traffic policeman, in his best hours at any rate, sees himself a commanding general. So shall you find a railway timekeeper who ranks himself with the sun, or a gardener setting out tulips and absorbed to the point of being a tulip himself; a master tailor dreaming, chalk in hand, over the lines of a pair of trousers; and then in one bold sweep carrying his dream into reality.

In this way do such workers reënter the lost kingdom of the world of the child where work and art are one. Life has its compensations.

Again there are those people who are said to "work," and spoken of as "working hard"—"working without ever taking a holiday"—"loving their work," etc.—who are not really working at all. A golf player doesn't work; a golf "pro" does. A leader of industry doesn't work; he's playing. A scientist—a real one—doesn't work, nor a real professor except now and again at such tasks as correcting examination papers or attending a students' banquet. I imagine that

Thomas Edison never did a day's work in his last fifty years.

.     .     .     .     .     .     .

The point is, therefore, that when a young man thinks out what he would like to do and to be, he reverts to the human impulse of wanting to do creative work, an activity that goes on for its own sake. Naturally many of them turn to the creative works of the arts—to be a poet, a writer, an actor, a playwright, an artist, or in our complex age, to be in "radio," or in the movies. I do not think that youth is tempted specially by the reward in money that goes with the highest measure of success in these things. As a matter of fact there is an evident measure of unfairness in the way in which the last little increment of higher talent or better luck brings an utterly disproportionate difference in pay. This aspect would on the whole repel youth, except the greedy, rather than attract it. The attraction lies in the creative character of the work itself. And of all such work that of the writer, needing no apparatus or appliance or adventitious aid other than a pencil and paper—oldest of all or at least dividing antiquity with the minstrel and the cave-picture man—may easily claim first place.

.     .     .     .     .     .     .

So then, one wants to "write," and that means to have, or get, ideas that are so interesting that if fully converted into words people want to read them—and will even (though we must pretend to forget that) pay money to read them. So the first inquiry is, How do you see about it to get ideas? Hence arises the question whether we get ideas by looking for them or by not looking for them; that is, by happening to be looking in another direction when they come along. In other words, is what is wanted in writing patient effort and conscientious industry? Or native genius and happy chance? This doesn't seem much of a question at first sight. But in reality it underlies all the discussion of how to write. John Stuart Mill once laid down a proposition so simple that it would require an idiot to deny it, namely that if you cultivate a piece of land more and more and better and better there comes a time when it isn't worth while to cultivate it better still. Having laid down this obvious truth, Mill declared it the most important proposition in Political Economy.

So with the question of whether to write by work or by inspiration. How *can* you be a writer by trying to be? You either are or you are not. "Poets," said the Romans, "are born, not made." So might you be inclined to believe till there comes the afterthought about the "mute inglorious Miltons" buried in the country churchyard, or the wish that you had seized and expressed the thoughts that have sometimes come to you, as you might have done if you had cultivated the power of expression.

We repeat then, Do *we,* or let us say, do authors, get ideas to write about by looking for them, or by looking in some other direction? There is no doubt that many things in life come to us by this latter process, at back rounds, so to speak. Happiness is one of them. Try to buy it, either by the yard (of dress) or by the quart (of champagne) and it slips away. Motion it aside while you are busy with duty and it will be there at your elbow.

I have often been struck by the width of the application of this principle. It is not possible to be a genial man by trying to, nor a dignified man, nor any other kind of man except the kind of man you really are. Yet there is also the contrary principle of the value of conscious effort. If we try hard to be or do something, not native to us, we may perhaps turn into something, or effect something, different but better. The man unsuccessfully attempting to be genial is at least pathetic and likable for his attempt.

Hence, when we turn to writing and literary work we find the same contrast between unsought effect and deliberate effort. Many writers, including poets, like to think, as we have said above, that a thing "comes to them," especially to have it come to them "in the woods" or "in the crowded mart" or in "the silent hours of the night." It seems bigger stuff than to have to go to it, or to have it arrive just after dinner. Our word "inspiration" embodies and elevates this idea. No doubt there is a sense in which ideas once started seem to develop themselves, in which a story falls into its place, effortless and inevitable.

But it is also true that writers, in the mass, would never get far without a great deal of deliberate effort, of conscious pursuit of an idea, of constant practise in suiting words to thought. My own experience has been confined to two fields, both of them aside from the main body of imaginative writing. I can therefore speak from personal experience only of a limited scope. It has been my lot to write a great deal of historical and political stuff, in which imagination only figures as the paint upon the gingerbread—the art of using language to interest and embellish thought. It would insult a historian to ask if he got his facts out of his own head.

But in my other small field, that of humorous writing, I think I know what I am talking about. A humorous *idea* that becomes the basis of a talk or story, most usually starts with some small casual incongruity of fact or language that crops up in ordinary life. A mind of a certain native angle of vision will see it where others don't, just as a hunter sees half-hidden game that others would pass unnoticed. A mind trained by practice to expression finds means to turn such small incongruity into something broad and visible, dragging after it perhaps a sequence.

For this, it seems to me, two things are needed—the native ability and the discipline of training. I believe that Horace has already thought of this—as of much else that I write—in saying *Doctrina vim promovet insitam.* (*Study calls out native power.*) I could give innumerable examples of this native genius for vision into the incongruities of *language,* or incongruities of fact. Robert Benchley, for example, sits down to write on India. He begins: "India! what mysteries does the name not suggest?" Ordinary people wouldn't see that anything has happened. But Benchley notes the incongruity of our language, when we ask, "What does it *not* do?" to mean that it does everything. Obviously, there are lots of mysteries that India does not suggest, says Benchley, such as the mystery of the lost Charlie Ross.

Or take again a case from the work of the late

Harry Graham. He talks of a country gentleman improving his house by putting in a billiard room which meant throwing the smoking room into the gun room. . . . Many people could live beside this phase, fast asleep. Not so Harry Graham. He sees at once the opportunity, as would no doubt any reader of these lines. But the ordinary reader might give a laugh to the phrase and yet he couldn't "carry on" with it as Harry Graham does, when he proceeds to throw the gun room into the dining room—a necessary consequence of the first throw—and then the butler's pantry into the scullery—and so on—till the whole place is a wreck.

So much for native ability to seize an opportunity that comes by chance. But what are we to say of the writer who sits down and struggles, even agonizes, to get something funny to write? Here we have Mr. A. A. Milne, whose native ability is at the saturation point, telling us in his autobiography of such struggles and agonies when he had to turn out his copy, week by week, for *Punch*. This seems very different from accident or inspiration. In reality, it is just the same thing. What Mr. Milne, and lesser people, are doing in this brute effort at being funny, is to run over in mental vision scenes and people with an eye and an ear on the watch. Something half-perceived and sub-consciously recorded is there as obvious as a partridge sitting on a bough. We have only to fire with both barrels. It may not be "sportsmanlike," in comparison with inspiration, but it gets the bird. Which leads us to the conclusion that getting ideas to write is much the same mixture of effort and accident as make, in general, the cross threads of the web of life.

.     .     .     .     .     .     .

We have decided then that writing has got to be done deliberately. We can't wait for it to come. On these terms, I claim that anybody can learn to write, just as anybody can learn to swim. Nor can anybody swim without learning how. A person can thus learn to swim up to the limits imposed by his aptitude and physique. The final result may not be worth looking at, but he can swim. So with writing. Nobody can learn to write without having learned how, either consciously or unconsciously. But it fortunately happens that what we call our education supplies to all of us the first basis for writing, the ability to read and to spell. Indeed our ordinary education, even in any elementary school, gives us a certain training in putting words together. Under the name of "composition" we go through a harrowing set of little exercises in correcting errors in the use of English; we put poetry back into prose, and go so far as to reach up to writing a composition on *An Autumn Walk,* or *The Fidelity of the Dog.* This is not "writing" in the sense adopted in this book but it is as essential a preliminary to it as learning to drive a nail into a board is to carpentry. People of exceptional native ability and no schooling sometimes write, and sometimes have reached great eminence without such training. But that is because the bent of their minds was so strong in that direction that unconsciously they weighed and measured words and phrases, fascinated with the power of expression, as an artistic genius, a young Giotto, with the pictured line.

Indeed, an ordinary environment of today gives us an even further start, and nowadays our sight and hearing through moving pictures, introduces us to a vast world of history, of actual events, and imaginary stories. These and the little circumstances of our own life give us plenty of material for thought. If we put our thoughts into words and write them down, that is *writing*. There's no more to it. It's just as simple as that.

In other words, anybody can write who has something to say and knows how to say it. Contrariwise, nobody can write who has nothing to say, or nothing that he can put into words.

Now it so happens that most of us have a good deal to say, but when we try to turn it into writing it gets muddled up by all kinds of preconceived ideas of how writing should be done, or is done by other people. So much so that when we write anything down it sounds false from start to finish. Each one of us is the custodian of *one* first class story, the story of his own life. Every human life is a story—is interesting if it can be conveyed. The poet Gray wrote down the "short and simple annals of the poor," sleeping under the elm trees of a country churchyard with such pathos and interest that they have lasted nearly two hundred years. But the poor couldn't have done it for themselves. Neither can we. We can't surround the story of our life with the majestic diction and the music of Gray's *Elegy*. But it is interesting, just the same, if we can tell it. Have you never noticed how at times people begin to tell you of their early life and early difficulties, and tell it utterly without affectation or effort, and how interesting it is in such form? Like this:

*Our farm was fifteen miles from a high school and it was too far to walk, and I didn't see how I could manage to go, and I couldn't have, but Uncle Al (he was the one who had gone out West) heard about it and he sent me fifty dollars and I started. I boarded Monday to Friday and walked home Fridays after school* . . . and so forth.

That's the way the man talks in an unguarded moment. But set him down to write out his life and see what happens. Either he sits and chews his pen and can't start, or he writes—with the result a hopeless artificiality. The same facts are there but dressed with a false adornment like ribbons on a beggar's coat. Something like this: *Our farm was situated some ten miles from the nearest emporium of learning, to wit, a high school, a distance beyond the range of Shanks' mare, the only vehicle within reach of my, or my family's, pecuniary resources* . . . etc., etc.

This failure happens because the man in question has been, unknowingly, taught how not to write. The necessarily somewhat artificial training of the schoolroom has led him unconsciously to think of writing as something elevated above ordinary speaking—like company manners. This knocks out at once the peculiar quality of "sincerity" which is the very soul of literature. "Sincerity" is the nearest word for what is meant; it implies not exactly honesty but a direct relation, a sort of inevitable relation as between the words used and the things narrated. This is the peculiar quality of many of the great writers who wrote without trying to write. Caesar wrote like this and John Bunyan, and better than all as an example is the matchless, simple Greek of the New Testament as put before us by King James's translators . . . *They were all with one accord in one place . . . and suddenly there came the sound as of a rushing mighty wind.* Or again: *And they said "Behold! There is a lad here that hath five barley loaves and three small fishes, but what are they among so many?" And he said, "Make the men sit down." And the men sat down, in number about five thousand. And there was much grass in the place . . .*

Now we can see from this the difficulty so many young people find when they try to "practise" writing. They are suddenly attempting to be someone else. Thus it often happens that when the conscious age of trying to write begins, young people use their correspondence with their friends as a form of practise. Ebenezer Smith, let us say, writes from Temagami camp a letter to a friend. Hitherto he had just written letters straight off, after this fashion: *We got the canoes into the water about five o'clock, just after the sun rose. The lake was dead calm and we paddled down to the portage in half an hour. I never saw the lake so calm.* But suddenly Ebenezer becomes sophisticated and when he sits down to write, the result is such a passage as this:

*A clear morning with just a faint sheen of mist before the sun kissed it away. I watched it vanish from the still surface of the lake and thought it seemed like some thin cerement, reverently drawn from the still face of death.* Oh, no, you didn't, Ebenezer! You thought that afterwards; stick to the canoe and portage stuff. It's more like Xenophon.

This collapse of Ebenezer Smith's correspondence as a method of beginning to write, leaves us still with the problem, how *do* you begin anyway? Where do you get the start and the practise?

We have just said that the ordinary education of the great mass of people, who go to school but don't go to college, supplies them with at least a sort of elementary beginning in "composition," in the expression of thought in words. What they get is at least something; indeed it is much. But it is mainly negative. It says what not to do. It tells them what errors to avoid. But you can't avoid anything if you are writing nothing. You must write first and "avoid" afterwards. A writer is in no danger of splitting an infinitive if he has no infinitive to split.

It might, therefore, be thought that in order to become a writer it is necessary to go on from school to college, and learn the "real stuff." Fortunately for the world at large this is not true. To go to college may be helpful but it is certainly not necessary. Writing is a thing which, sooner or later, one must do for oneself, of one's own initiative and energy. Those who are debarred from the privilege of attending college may take courage. The college kills writers as well as makes them. It is true that a gifted professor can do a lot; he can show the way, can explain what are the things in literature that the world has found great and why, in his opinion, they are so. Better still, he can communicate his own enthusiasm, and even exalt his pupils on the wings of his own conceit. More than that, the college gives companionship in study; it is hard to work alone, harder still to enjoy. Appreciation grows the more it is divided.

But as against all that, college training carries the danger of standardized judgments, of affected admiration, of the pedantry of learning. Students read with one eye, or both, on the examination, classify and memorize and annotate till they have exchanged the warm pulsation of life for the *post-mortem* of an inquest.

But the main point is that writing, whether done in and by college or without a college, has got to be done for and by oneself. If you want to write, start and write down your thoughts. If you haven't any thoughts, don't write them down. But if you have, *write* them down; thoughts about anything, no matter what, in your own way, with no idea of selling them or being an author. Just put down your thoughts. If later on it turns out that your thoughts are interesting and if you get enough practise to be able to set down what they really are in language that conveys them properly—the selling business comes itself. There are many things in life, as we have said, that come to us as it were "at back rounds." Look for happiness and you find dust. Look for "authorship" and you won't find it; look for self-expression in words, for its own sake, and an editor's check will rustle down from Heaven on your table. Of course you really *hoped* for it; but you won't get it unless and until self-expression for its own sake breaks through.

What do you write about? You write about anything. Your great difficulty will be, as soon as you apprehend this method, that you can *think* things but can't say them. Most people live and die in that state; their conversation is stuffed with smothered thought that can't get over.

Take an example: Two people are walking out with the crowd from the roar and racket of a football game, just over. One says, "I don't know that I quite believe in all that rooting stuff, eh?" And the other answers, reflectively, "Oh, I don't know; I'm not so sure." That's as far as they can get. What the first man means is that organized hysteria is a poor substitute for spontaneous enthusiasm; and what the other means is that after all even genuine enthusiasm *unless* organized, unless given the aid of regularity and system—even spontaneous enthusiasm degenerates into confusion; our life, itself artificial, compels a certain "organization." They can't say this, but either of these two spectators would read with pleasure a well-written magazine article under such a title as *Should Rooting be Rooted Out?* The articles we think really good are those that express the things that we think but can't say.

Now when people begin to write down their thoughts, some of them will find that their thoughts take the form of *judgments,* of opinions on things that are. Others will find that their thoughts instinctively run into fancies, that is, ideas of things that *might* happen, and these become stories. Stories are just new editions of what might happen to somebody based on what did happen to somebody else. Hence, for many people the desire to write assumes the form of a sort of wish, or instinct to write "stories" . . . They turn with impatience from all talk of preparation, of practice, of words. All that seems artificial. The natural idea, to them, is to try to write a story and then try to sell it to a magazine; and thus by practice learn how to write and get paid for it at the same time.

That is all very well. But it is not for you or me. It is only a person of a higher determination, or of a tougher hide than yours or mine who can pursue that path. The refusal of a first manuscript, to certain sensitive natures, such as yours and mine, comes as such a crushing blow to self-confidence and self-belief that there is a danger that it may annihilate all further attempts. Charles Dickens, in one of his happiest passages, talks of the tears that came to his eyes when for the first time in life he saw his accepted manuscript in print. "I walked down to Westminster Hall and turned into it for half an hour, because my eyes were so dimmed with joy and pride that they could not bear the street."

But let someone else tell us of the unrecorded, the hidden tears shed over the manuscript that was not accepted, the story that came back. From one such disappointment the aspirant may recover, from a second —from a third—but not from many. Few beginners can realize how little editorial refusal of a manuscript really means. Editors are beset by all kinds of conditions and limitations as to space, as to what they have on hand already, as to the particular type of story (apart from merit) that they propose to use—or that their proprietors propose to use, as to scenes, settings, as to God knows what—things that a young aspirant towards writing would never dream of. He thinks that if his story is good, the editors *must* take it. He doesn't realize that the editors may have decided that they have accepted enough stories about love to last six months, that they can't use rich widows for a year, have definitely decided never to use Negro dialect, and can't run anything more that has to do with the sea— or with the land—or with religion—till they've used all the sea and the land and the religion they've bought already. But of course no one beginning literary work has any idea of this.

Some beginners in writing, it is true, seem to have an inkling of this that gives them an indifference to rejection, or to have a hardy courage or a strength of self-belief that lets them rise superior to editorial discouragement. I have known a few such. A friend and contemporary of mine who turned out to be one of the most successful crime story writers of our day has told me that before he had a single story accepted he had written enough crime to fill all the penitentiaries. Another one of the best known and most honored of Canadian writers says that he had enough rejection slips from editors to paper a room before he ever sold anything. But such an arduous path is not for you and me.

It is more reasonable to suppose that most beginners underestimate the difficulty of story-telling. What they write at first is not apt to be really worth a selling price. It is a pity to stake their literary future on their first efforts. Few people begin at their best, or even at their average level. The exceptions, such as Rudyard Kipling, who began at the top, with what seems effortless excellence— Well, they're exceptional.

Stories, I repeat, that are really worth while, are hard to write. Most people who aspire to be story writers think that stories depend upon incidents, upon a plot. This is not so. They depend on the telling. As to incident or plot, there are fundamentally only three of them, that So-and-So was born, that he fell in love and got married, that he died—with the variation that he fell in love and didn't get married, and that he nearly died but didn't. Stories about how a man nearly died and didn't are called *Adventure Stories,* and stories about how a person got married, or didn't, are called *Love Stories.* But the main thing in any story is to be able to *think* the character into reality, and then find the words to convey what you think. Once you can create a character, as the phrase runs (*catch* a character would be better), anything and everything about him is a story.

Now you may feel very vividly that there's a character to be caught but you've got to catch him first. There is a waiter, let us say, in a restaurant you frequent, whom you feel to be a regular character. But saying that won't make him one. You've got to catch and convey something about him that makes him one, and then you don't need to tell your reader that the waiter is a character. He'll say so first. What makes so many stories stupid and unreadable is that the writer instead of making characters, announces them. He says, "The waiter was one of the quaintest characters whom our hero had ever looked upon." Was he? But we don't see him. Or else the writer thinks to succeed by piling up an accumulation of details so that the sum total must at least come to something. But this, except to fill space against a price, is all wrong. The best descriptions are the shortest; their point is in their effective suggestion; the reader does the rest. The best lesson in this respect is to learn to admire and linger on the work of others; if it is true that Shakespeare (so he said) often found himself "admiring this man's work and that man's scope," there is no doubt that the process helped to make him Shakespeare.

. . . . . . .

We are still talking then of how to begin. I would like to offer as a practical suggestion the keeping of a sort of "commonplace book" in which one writes all kinds of random attempts at expression. If you have just read a book write a few words down about it. If a moving picture has deeply moved you, write down the fact and try to explain why. Cultivate admiration of other people's words and phrases that seem to express much, and write them down. Soon you will write your own. In a certain sense all literature begins with imitation. Divergence comes later.

It is often thought that writing a diary is *par excellence* the most natural and effective way to begin writing. I don't think so at all. A diary is apt to throw the person on the wrong track. It tends to be such an artificial business. What are you to put in it—all your most intimate thoughts? But most people haven't got any, or none that they care to put on paper. The young heroine in novels spreads out her diary and tells it that it is to be her dearest friend. "I will put into it, my dear diary," she says, "all that I think, all that I feel, all that I don't know." It sounds a large order. In reality it only means that this is the author's way of writing the book, by pretending that the heroine wrote it.

On the other hand, if a diary is written as a simple record of what happens, done in the writer's own ordinary language, it is apt to be of no great value as literary practice. Example: diary of J. Smith, on vacation:

*July 8: went bass fishing: got six. July 9: didn't go bass fishing: lake too rough: played poker: lost a dollar twenty. July 10: bass fishing: didn't get any,—*

Nor would it make it any better if J. Smith used his diary for the kind of fits of affectation described already in connection with correspondence:—

July 8th. *We went out to fish for bass, the lake a beautiful amethyst gray, very calm as if stilled into expectancy. Our piscatorial efforts were rewarded by the capture of six bass, the largest of which we could easily see without the need of scales, to represent a weight of five pounds, at least, while all possessed a beauty of shimmering colour, a length of fin and a breadth of jaw characteristic of the large-mouthed black bass (ranunculus silva) at its largest.*

On the whole, therefore, I think we may say goodbye to diary-making and personal correspondence as methods of beginning to write.

But let us come back for the moment and take the other alternative of the dilemma spoken of above. Suppose a would-be writer can't begin. I really believe there are many excellent writers who have never written because they never could begin. This is especially the case of people of great sensitiveness, or of people of advanced education. Professors suffer most of all from this inhibition. Many of them carry their unwritten books to the grave. They overestimate the magnitude of the task; they overestimate the greatness of the final result. A child in a "prep" school will write "The History of Greece" and fetch it home finished after school. "He wrote a fine History of Greece the other day," says his proud father. Thirty years later the child, grown to be a professor, dreams of writing the History of Greece—the whole of it from the first Ionic invasion of the Aegean to the downfall of Alexandria. But he dreams. He never starts. He can't. It's too big.

Anybody who has lived around a college knows the pathos of these unwritten books. Moreover, quite apart from the non-start due to the appalling magnitude of the subject, there is a non-start from the mere trivial difficulty of "how to begin" in the smaller sense, how to frame the opening sentences. In other words how do you get started?

The best practical advice that can be given on this subject is, don't *start*. That is, don't start anywhere in particular. Begin at the end: begin in the middle, but *begin*. If you like you can fool yourself by pretending that the start you make isn't really the beginning and that you are going to write it all over again. Pretend that what you write is just a note, a fragment, a nothing. Only get started.

.   .   .   .   .   .

So let us get this book started in the next chapter.

# CHAPTER II

## THE LAWS OF GRAMMAR AND FREE SPEECH

*Good society and bad grammar — Grammar has no
rights which the writer is bound to respect — Usage
rules — Whose usage? — Where the McGregor sits is
the head of the table — But who is McGregor? —
Grammar follows, not leads — Not a prescription, but
a post-mortem — The tyranny of authority — The
French Academy — English free speech — The revolt
of the pronouns; Are these they? Or is that them? —
The massacre of the suffixes — The insurrection of the
split infinitive — Outlawed words; Have you only got
a tendency to write like Shakespeare wrote?*

As said in the preceding chapter, each of us has had
at school a sort of preliminary training in the correct
use of language. We are taught to distinguish between
what is "good grammar" and what is "bad grammar"
—a phrase which is probably itself "bad grammar."
Some celebrated person in England once said, "I cannot conceive that the study of grammar is of the slight-
est use to people who have always mixed in good society." I forget who said it, but it was one of those
things which, once said, seems to *stick* and to be kept
alive by repetition. One may compare it with the famous utterance which Molière puts into the mouth of
one of his characters: "People of quality know everything without having ever learned anything." It also

suggests a certain English magazine of the late nineties of last century that was founded "to be written for gentlemen by gentlemen."

But even if the study of grammar has no meaning for people who have always moved in good society it has plenty of meaning for those of us who always haven't, or have moved in plenty of bad as well. We can appreciate the service performed by the "laws of grammar" towards the stability of language, by turning to look at what happens to language when it heads away from the law. I refer to the unrestrained language of grammarless people, exuberant in its very errors. No better example of this can be found than in the reproductions of it which the late Ring W. Lardner used to love to weave into the dialogue of his stories. Lardner, whose relatively early death cut short a literary career in its full course, was a great humourist, and like many great humourists he found the chief source of his humour in plain truth; not in exaggeration, but in setting forth life and character exactly as it is, with just enough of unseen selection and omission to set what he selected in a high light. A part of such a method involved the reproduction of the natural speech of plain people—humorous in its contact with correct language, and with its mock dignity on a printed page.

Here, in evidence, are a couple of sentences taken from a little story of great simplicity and charm (*The Golden Honeymoon*), recounting the golden wedding holiday tour of an aged couple, midway between rich and poor, but a long way from wealth of language.

They meet fortuitously another old couple, acquaintances of long ago. Only Ring Lardner could put so much into so little—so much of character, interesting because it is not that of one old man but of millions—of retrospect, not of two old couples but of all old couples. He does it by letting them talk, the old man as a narrator.

. . . . . . .

Reunion of old friends:
*Then they came over and hunted us up and I will confess I wouldn't of known him. Him and me is the same age to the month, but he seems to show it more some way.*

Description of a Public Amusement Park:
*In the middle they's a big bandstand and chairs for the folks to set and listen to the concerts which they give you music for all tastes, from "Dixie" up to classical pieces like "Hearts and Flowers." Then all around they's places marked off for different sports and games —chess and checkers and dominoes for folks that enjoys those kind of games.*

But for the full appreciation of this exquisite humour we must refer the reader to the story itself. We are only dealing here with its bearing on the use and application of rules of grammar.

. . . . . .

One may imagine a school teacher writing up these sentences on the blackboard, with the words, "Correct the errors in the above sentences." Once corrected there would be—or shall we say "they'd be"—little left for the author's purpose.

.    .    .    .    .    .

It is clear that the writer, or speaker, of these sentences has the grammatical forms all wrong. Here is *him* used as the subject of a sentence, and *me* along with it, although these forms do not belong with the nominative case, but are reserved for the objective. Here is the verb *is* used in place of *are,* in other words a singular form in place of a plural. Here is *they* instead of *there* and *wouldn't of* instead of *wouldn't have,* mistakes that arise from mixing up the sound and the spelling of similar words. Here is the phrase *concerts which they give you music for all tastes*—in which the logic of language collapses in a heap. Who gives which to what?

.    .    .    .    .    .

But let it be noted that ever so many people who use what is called cultivated speech and who would not make any of the above errors, would be quite unable to talk of them as "cases," and "numbers" and such, having long ago forgotten what such things are, or having never understood them. This brings us back to the grammar of people in good society.

.    .    .    .    .    .

Now we can realize from the quotations above into what an exuberant overgrowth, into what a tangle of conflicting forms, living language would have grown if there had been no grammarians and logicians to clip and prune and trim it. We can understand how and why, in the days before printing set language into a mould, speech broke and disintegrated into dialects that became mutually unintelligible. The printer and the grammarian, the spelling book and the logician have all been among the servants of humanity; nor to any part of humanity more so than to the British and the American nations in whose unity of language, whose mutual comprehension lies a principal hope for world salvation. But even at that we must remember that servants must never move up from the servants' hall to the higher table. We must realize that the rules of grammar and such formal regulations of what we may say and write rest for the most part on usage, that is, on what we actually *do* say, and do write.

In a certain broad sense, no doubt, the form and sequence of language is based on reason and logic but this is only true in the general and not of necessity in the particular. An accepted form may be quite contrary to the logic of thought, and yet carry its meaning without any ambiguity. Who, except by pedantic ingenuity, could make logic of such forms as "John was given a stick." "This is a thing we could do with more of." Sometimes an illogical form is accepted in one language as correct and even commendable and in another is supposed to be a vulgar usage. "I have never seen nobody" ought logically to mean "I have always been within sight of somebody." Instead of that it is just an emphatic form of saying "I have never seen anybody," and is bad English but excellent French and admirable Greek. For emphasis' sake, language breaks away from tenses, substituting present forms for past, as when we say "He enters, what does he see? A lifeless body on the floor." But we don't mean that this is going on now. We mean that it happened in the past. The change of tense makes it vivid; it seems to happen again. Accepted usage, even admired usage, often breaks away in the form of metaphor and hyperbole, from truth and even from consistency. We talk of people being "bathed in tears" or "drowned in grief" or "crushed with sorrow." Where is a man standing when he is "beside himself with excitement"? If a man near him has "one foot in the grave" where is the other? And if a third man is present but is "wrapped up in himself," where is he lying round? No wonder children find it hard to understand the talk of grown-up people.

. . . . . . .

Hence, what we call correct grammar, correct language, and recognized syntax, depends really upon usage and upon who does the using. People who start to study grammar in the formal sense, and people who try to learn to write by beginning in that way, are apt to be misled. They get the idea that there exists a set of rules which must not be broken, of forms which must, or must not, be used. They get the further idea that correct forms of language have to be logical and consistent, but in reality there is no test but that of usage. Grammar is only an analysis after the facts, a post-mortem on usage. Usage must come first and usage must rule. The only difficulty is to *know* whose usage. The answer is obviously the usage of the best writers; this leads to the further difficulty of knowing who are the best writers. We find them to be the writers recognized as the best by the best people. With that we are again getting dangerously near writing done by gentlemen for gentlemen. The search for a final authority thus becomes as difficult as the search for a first cause in physics.

Various nations, or rather, the "people of quality" of various nations, have often tried to establish a fixed authority as to what should be correct language and approved literature. One thinks of the famous example of the French Academy, a royal institution founded under the fostering care of Cardinal Richelieu. Its forty members were supposed to be the chief literary men of France, its judgment in criticism final, and its "Dictionary" the guardian of the French language against perversion or deterioration. It took sixty years to produce its first dictionary (1694). The Academy, as organized, perished in the French Revolution but came to life again (1796) and lived (till 1939) as the language and literature section of the Institute of France, to which its name was commonly transferred.

For the English language, the people of Britain and America have not, and never have had any such constituted authority as the French Academy. We have as our standards various dictionaries of high repute, from the lexicon of Dr. Johnson down. We have the standard called the King's English though no one knows where to find it; such centres of authority as Harvard or Oxford; and a whole library of text books. But none of these things has the authority of the French Academy. These are not sovereigns, these are umpires. An umpire doesn't make the rules.

. . . . . . .

One can realize what is apt to happen as the result of setting up authoritative standards by recalling what happened in France. Literature under academic control began to conform to set patterns. The drama, for instance, had to follow the noble lead given to it by Racine and Corneille. It had to remain "elevated." It must deal with noble and distinguished characters, such as Achilles, Iphigenia, and Beelzebub. Its scene must be a court or a palace or a temple; its language the stately periods of classical metre—sonorous, regular, each thought complete within its allotted space.

Now noble subjects are noble subjects and regularity is pleasing and symmetry is symmetrical. But even of a good thing there can be too much. Uniformity gets wearisome. The ornaments become fetters, the symmetry that of a prison wall. Hence, presently came the great revolt in France against the classical drama. There was the terrific excitement, almost a free fight, over the production of Victor Hugo's *Hernani* (1830). Here was a play which abandoned Achilles and Beelzebub in favor of a Spanish bandit, and which defied all the laws of metre by actually running the sense over from one line till the next. By the time the excitement had died down French literature had broken out of its academic prison and was loose on the streets.

Even earlier in the same epoch Walter Scott had discovered that if you were writing in English you needn't write about Julius Caesar or Desdemona provided you had a Highland chieftain and a girl in a tartan. Then presently Charles Dickens found that even if you had only a gin shop and a debtors' prison you could find literature in it somwhere.

Thus did literature emancipate itself from authority

and fixed models, still preserving a real or pretended reverence for the higher models of Greece.

.     .     .     .     .     .     .

It is proper to remind ourselves at this point of the bearing of this discussion of authority on the question of how to write. It bears thus: Every young writer must decide for himself whether he is trying to walk in old paths or find new ones, to cultivate the style of the recognized writers or to manufacture a style for himself. Obviously, there are difficulties both ways. Too much imitation is like a monkey at a looking-glass. But innovation for innovation's sake is like a monkey without a looking-glass. In other words, it is just silly. Witness the great quantities of "free verse" written anyhow and anyway, just to be different, and succeeding in being as "free" as the dancing fancy of a lunatic. Novelty is not in itself merit. A *new* word may be a very poor word, taking the place of a better one.

Yet on the other hand mere imitation and repetition fall asleep. China folded its hands and fell asleep over its primitive books thousands of years ago till the very sleep made the books sacred. It is possible perhaps that we have fallen asleep over Greek and Latin; that we are dozing off over the long rolling sentences of the Gibbons and the Macaulays, as resonant as the sound of the sea; that our rules of grammar are gradually setting like cement. If so, the first thing for a writer to do is to wake up, to break loose from authority and convention.

.     .     .     .     .     .     .

It is doubtful then whether the attempt at authoritative control is of real benefit to national language and literature. In the history of letters, as in the history of political development, there is the same age-long struggle between liberty and despotism, or, as others see it, between license and order. The attempt to lay down rules of grammar, canons of taste, laws of the paragraph will provoke rebellion as surely as a decree of the Star Chamber or the provisions of the Stamp Act. The man who first splits an infinitive is as bold a rebel as the man who cracks a skull. The abolition of English suffixes was as great a triumph as the abolition of English serfdom. The levelling out of our English plurals into s. was as glorious an advance as the overthrow of the *strong* verb (. . . *sang* . . . *swam* . . . *ran* . . .) by the *weak,* the ones with the past tense in -ed—such as *I skidded,* instead of *I scud* —which now hold almost the whole field and apply to all the new additions. In our own day we have witnessed, or are witnessing the final suppression of the subjunctive, and the confused revolt of the pronouns.

   .    .    .    .    .    .    .

Even at that there still remains for each of us the question how much of the change is good, how much is bad. Where does change become mere senseless destruction? Each of us, in accepting changes of grammar, will be inclined to go a little beyond what was current in his youth, and then pause just as the youthful radical slowly passes into the elderly conservative. For the individual, innovation runs out. Personally, I find that I strongly object to such changes as the use of "due" instead of "owing," a thing unknown in my youth. I objected, but have long since forgotten it, to the use of the vocative *Oh,* in calling out to anybody

*"Oh, Bill," "Oh, Jim,"* instead of the simple if sudden call of *"Bill"* or *"Jim"* as current in the England of my childhood.

.        .        .        .        .        .        .

But all such decisions about changes to be accepted or refused stand on a different ground from the rooted objections of grammarians to any change at all, the attempt to set up a formal authority, to prevent language from degenerating. The real source of this attitude was the belief so widely held by scholars until our own day that modern languages *were* degenerating, in fact that they had steadily degenerated from the stately classical languages; that French and Spanish were broken-down languages, a sort of wreckage still constantly tending to disintegrate, and English a sort of peasant dialect that never had the early advantage of a Latin origin, but had come up by being blended with French and by being buttressed by Latin, like a workhouse boy steadily improved by Sunday-school until almost fit to associate with the quality.

The truth is all the other way. It is, of course, an act of literary heresy to say it but there is to my mind no doubt about the superiority of the English language over any and every ancient tongue. Language undergoes progress. Scholars, we know, can still go into ecstasies over Greek, the more so as they have their ecstasies to themselves. They show us the subtlety of Greek in its having not two numbers, singular and plural, but three—singular, dual and plural. The dual means two people. "I love" is singular; "we love" is plural; but "we two love" is dual—as snug for lovers as love itself. Yet to me the distinction merely suggests the uncertain counting of a hen, or the primitive races who count, *One, two, three—a whole lot,* and let it go at that.

Yet it is only fair to remember that people of such wide reading and such marvellous command of language as Macaulay have acknowledged, indeed have taken for granted, the superiority of Greek. Macaulay can find no higher praise for our language than to say that it is "inferior to the tongue of Greece alone."

In such a matter there is, also, no tribunal or court of reference. Very few people now study Greek; fewer still succeed in learning it. The few who claim to *know* Greek literature in Greek hug their knowledge to their hearts like a child with a rag doll; thus does each of us with such poor things as are our own. So there is no one to tell the world that language has vastly improved in the last two thousand years. Scholars could weep over the intrusion of the preposition to obliterate the Latin ablative case, over the intrusion of auxiliary verb, in reality as handy as the adjustable parts of an up-to-date machine. Greek often said in one word what we say in four. But so does Zulu.

The elaborate forms and suffixes for cases, numbers, moods and tenses in Greek and Latin are primitive and clumsy. You will find them, or similar things, in the Bantu or the Ojibway or any primitive speech. As beside our easy and flexible system of indicating the connection of things by means of prepositions as connecting words, they are nowhere. Even a person quite unacquainted with philology and language study will understand what is meant if he will permit a simple example. In English we still have a few surviving broken-off forms that can be tacked on anywhere just like a Latin or a Zulu suffix. We can use the "wards" in *homewards, landwards, seawards,* etc., or in a new combination, let us say, *townwards* and find it intelligible. We can say, he went London-wards or Kentwards, or shore-wards. Still more alive is the suffix "less." *He came into the room, hatless, coatless, breathless, almost pantless.* We could turn the suffix *less*—if we wanted to set the clock backwards and "go Latin" (or go Zulu)—into a case and call it the *Separative Case.* Grammarians would then talk of the *subtlety* of the *Separative Case* as used to show that the thing indicated is not there, such as *pantless*—having no pants. But why such a word is superior to *without any pants* it is hard to see.

·    ·    ·    ·    ·    ·    ·

So much then for the idea that the breaking and shifting of English in the past was a form of degeneration. It was progress, and if we recognized this fact it means that we need not seek in ancient languages models for our own. A thing is not correct because it is classical. A rule is not binding because it bound Julius Caesar. The question then is—where are we to look for guidance as to correct English?

·    ·    ·    ·    ·    ·    ·

Any student looking into a technical book on errors in the use of English will be apt to find himself badly perplexed. There seems to be a standing contrast between the forms of speech which we commonly use and the forms required by the rules of grammar. This is especially so in the case of our pronouns. If anybody calls out "Who is there?" most of us would answer

"Me!" or "It's me." The *rule* demands "I," on the ground that this is a nominative case after a copulative (or coupling) verb. But the French language forgot about this copulative verb centuries ago and all French people say, *C'est moi*. This grammatical point was made a focus of fun in the once favorite comedy *Ici on parle français* (the shop-sign for "French spoken here.") A customer entering the shop asks, *"Qui est la personne ici qui parle français?"* The young man behind the counter bows deeply and answers *"Je."* The audience gives him a laugh but the English grammarian would give him a medal.

Suppose anybody said to you, "Have you seen my scissors anywhere about?" and you pointed to a pair of scissors on a table, would you say, "Are these they?" and would the person say, "Yes, thank you, those are they"? Surely not. "That's them," is as familiar and honest as it is incorrect under the rule.

The truth is that our English pronouns are a disorderly and drunken lot. We no sooner straighten them up on one side than they fall over on the other. Take the case of the wide-spread, and still spreading, tendency to use *I* instead of *me*. "He gave a present to Mary and I."—"He came over to see Sis and I." This "error," if it is one, may have existed forever so long but of late years it has spread like a weed in a neglected garden. I think the explanation is very simple. People were taught at school that they mustn't say, as they were inclined to say in their home talk, "me and Mary went to the village." They must put *Mary* first for politeness' sake, and put *I* for *me* for grammar's sake. "Mary and I went to the village." It sounded affected but they knew it was correct. The lesson was learned too well. People lost track of what they learned at school about the subject of a verb and the object of a verb, *me* being the form for the object, and lumped the phrase *Mary and I* together as high-class English, subject, object, or anything. It is not really a case of a weed of error in a neglected garden. It is a grammatical plant gone wrong from over-watering.

. . . . . . .

The difficulties of our pronouns drive some modest people to try to get out of using them at all. Compare the case of those who avoid *me and Mary* and *Mary and I* by saying, *Mrs. J. and self* . . . or observe the queer use of "one" as a substitute for "I," much in vogue among English people in such sentences as: *Of course one finds oneself very much at home in Canada. One sees so many things that one has always been used to* . . . etc. I don't know whether this is modesty or affectation. The trouble is that it is very hard to find the answering dialogue to fit it. Are you to say, *Would one like a cigar or does one prefer cigarettes?*

The same pronoun *one* is used in British journalism, not in ours in North America, as a fitting form for the use of interviewers, reporters, writing up an occasion or a person, and, as it were, remaining themselves in a sort of mist of obscurity, or anonymity.

*One entered the great man's room. One felt oneself at once in the presence of a man of exception. Here was one whom one felt was born to command,* etc. . . .

This form may be dictated by self-effacement. But

I see little to recommend it. The Japanese "humble worm" is better.

.     .     .     .     .     .     .

But the difficulties connected with the use of pronouns are only one case of what has been called the "common perplexities" of our everyday language. As with the pronouns, many of these perplexities resolve themselves on examination into a struggle between pedantry and common sense. If "pedantry" is too harsh a word let us call it orthodoxy.

Consider such so-called errors as "Have you got any money?" "We haven't got the time! What have you got?" Authority tries to cast out the word got from such sentences as a policeman turns out a loafer; but in vain; its friends bring it back and insist on keeping it. "Don't you see," says the pedant, "that all you need say is 'Have you any money?'" The word got isn't necessary, or, if you like a longer word for it, it is "pleonastic." Whereon the pedant warms to his task with a whole section on pleonasm and tautology (Greek for too much and the same thing over again). After which people go on using *got,* because they haven't got any faith in the rule.

The people are in this case, I think, quite right. It is true that the verb *"have"* possesses a full meaning of its own in the sense of possess or hold.

*Now, infidel, I have thee on the hip.*

But a thousand years ago, in English as in French, it also acquired a weaker use as an auxiliary, meaning an assistant word. Thus in Latin, as the language "broke down" into French, instead of saying *I killed him,* they could say *I have him killed.* This marked off a new tense with gradations of meaning not indicated before. We can appreciate these gradations by considering the difference between, *I have him licked* and *I have licked him*.

But in language as elsewhere one can't be master and servant both. In proportion as *have* served for an auxiliary it lost force as an independent unit. It needed support itself. Hence it drew to it the word "got" and keeps it in a pleonastic partnership. *I have got some money* meant at first *obtained some money* and then simply, *I have some money*. Note again the shading that lies between *Have you got your money?* and *Have you got your railway ticket?* This latter query could mean *purchased* or *obtained* and so it stands even more easily, half on its own feet, half leaning.

The conclusion is that in many expressions the addition of *got* lends force or emphasis. Common sense justifies it.

To take another example. All the text books warn us that the word *like* must not be used as a conjunction. We are allowed to say *He is like his father* but we must not say *He talks like his father talks*. We are not to say *I wish I could play the ukulele like John does*. We are to say *I wish I could play the ukulele as John does*—either that or not wish at all—and don't play the ukulele. If we insist on doing so we must find some different way of expressing the same thing. Thus in the first illustration above we would be told *He talks as his father talks,* would not sound complete and that it would be better to use some such phrase as —*His manner of talking is similar to that usual with his father*. This everlasting desire to "recast" for "recasting's" sake recalls the quaint attitude towards the French language adopted by one of my Upper Canada College pupils of fifty years ago. He appeared deeply impressed with the feebleness of French speech. "How do you say in French," I asked him, "Give me some bread?" "You can't say it," he answered. "You have to say something else."

So with the grammarians and such terms as *like* as a conjunction; you have to say something else. Yet as a matter of fact most people, and even grammarians on a vacation, use *like* in this way all the time. So do the best authors, at least the ones with the keenest sense of what words mean as apart from rules as to what they ought to mean. Here is Charles Dickens writing to his friend John Forster (Jan. 7, 1841) in regard to the death (at his own hands, or rather at his own pen) of his Little Nell: "Nobody will miss her like I shall." If you had told Dickens that he ought to write, "Nobody will miss her *as* I shall," he would have objected at once—would have said that it wasn't strong enough.

The reason is not far to seek. *Like* is a living word, with a meaning in it. *As* is a dead word, a mere convention, a symbol. Once no doubt *as* was a living word —no doubt one could find a meaning for it in an Anglo-Saxon dictionary, but not for us. But *like* is not only alive but is a word that has carried down with it through the centuries an intensity of significance. It meant originally "a corpse," it still does in German (*Leichnam*). The little gate with a roof in front of English country churches is called a *lych* gate (corpse gate). There rested the corpse, waiting for the clergyman. To realize how "corpse" turned to "like" consider such phrases as *the dead image of a person. This is the dead image of John. This is John's like. This is like John.*

No wonder then that people instinctively use a phrase such as "to write like Shakespeare does." They can feel the comparison in the word.

One of the latest victims to fall into disrepute with the rule makers is the word *only*. We are told that we must not say, *I only had ten cents.* We are told that *only* must stand before the particular word or phrase which it numerically qualifies. *Washington had only three thousand men . . . The laundry comes only on Friday.* But as a matter of fact ordinary people are apt to distribute *only* much more freely. In many cases indeed the varying position of the *only* marks a varying shade of sense which the speaker or writer instinctively feels. At times it falsifies the true meaning to put *only* in what looks at first sight its qualifying place. Compare, *This is a tale only told to children,* and *This is a tale told only to children.* In the first case *told-to-children* becomes one solidified idea and the arrangement has more meaning. Compare again: *This out of the way village is only explored by snow-shoe clubs.* Here it would be quite wrong to put *is explored only by snow-shoe clubs.* In reality it is not *explored* at all. The point of the sentence is the arrangement, meaning that snow-shoe clubs come upon it as explorers might come upon something.

Similarly a great deal of over-sweeping condemnation is directed against the so-called split infinitive, meaning the insertion of words in between *to* and the infinitive verb with which it is associated. Thus Hamlet might have said, "To be or to not be," but he had evidently taken first year English at the Court of Denmark and said, "To be or not to be." But in and of itself there is nothing erroneous, or ill-sounding or illogical about a split infinitive. Many of our actual verbs are in themselves split infinitives as when we say "to undertake" and "to overthrow." In daily speech people split infinitives as readily as they split profits. Many of us who write books are quite willing to split an infinitive or to half split it or quite split it according to effect. We might even be willing to sometimes so completely, in order to gain a particular effect, split the infinitive as to practically but quite consciously run the risk of leaving the *to* as far behind as the lost caboose of a broken freight train. All we need admit is that many split infinitives are clumsy and purposeless and need bandaging.

But taking things all in all, the student who wishes to write need pay but little attention to the question of grammar. Such rules mainly consist in telling us what not to say. No writer can get far on that. Eloquent silence is not literature.

Far different is the matter of the choice of words and of the construction of sentences. A first requisite and a constant aid to good writing is the cultivation of a feeling towards the words we use, an appreciation of their significance, of the distinctions of their meanings and of the peculiar colour, the shades of meaning, that surround so many of them. This last is the most important of all.

## CHAPTER III

## THE MYSTERY AND MAGIC OF WORDS

*The superiority of English to all dead, half dead and living languages — Its troubled history — The Saxon base and the layers laid over it — Saxon for simplicity, for home and hearth and love in the gloaming — Norman French for cuisine and chivalry — Church Latin for saints and the devil — Book Latin for the printer's devil — Greek for metaphysics — The world's tribute of words, Dutch yachts, China tea and Moslem muslin — All elements still active as when a lounge-lizard speaks over the telephone to a piece of calico*

OUR English is a beautiful language. It is as far superior to the other languages as those who speak it, British and American, are to other peoples. It has had a long and troubled history. Those who spoke it in its earlier form were overwhelmed by foreigners; their language was submerged but survived. It had thus all the advantages of early adversity. The French say that one must suffer in order to be beautiful, and this may be applied to languages. English, after foreign mishandling of its elaborate suffixes and its clumsy forms, emerged into the beauty of its present simplicity.

Everybody knows something of the origins of English and there are admirable manuals available for its study. We need here only refer to it in outline. Our language in its earliest form, as spoken by Angles and Saxons, was a part of the great Aryan or Indo-European speech that swept slowly across Europe in the centuries before our written history began. As it moved it broke and disintegrated into many varieties, nor did the division of language necessarily keep on corresponding with race in the physical sense. Language was often superimposed on a conquered people or acquired by an alien one. The notion that the languages of Europe corresponded to physical races is as old as the German philologist Max Müller, and as forgotten. We might as well infer from the talk of negroes that they are a black branch of the Anglo-Saxons. Thus the Normans were Norsemen who acquired French in Normandy and Italian in Lombardy. A fringe of Western European people were not even Aryan at all. Certain broken fragments, languages like the Basque, remain to prove it.

It used to be the general understanding that the Angles and Saxons invaded England under Hengist and Horsa in 449 A.D. But modern scholarship is now inclined to class Hengist and Horsa with Romulus and Remus, and Damon and Pythias, as types not men. But at any rate the Angles and Saxons came. The Romans had already left.

The Britons were driven westward and northward in an unending war of centuries. There was no amalgamation of languages. The Angles and Saxons took over here and there words left by the Romans. Some of these were names for things they didn't have at home, such as *street* and *camp* and *wine*. Others were place-names many of which became so battered in the course of centuries that the original Latin can no longer be recognized on the surface. *Eboracum* turned to *Eborcum, Borcum, Borc, York*. After the conversion of the Anglo-Saxons to Christianity, priests from Rome brought in the Latin that went with the service of the church—*minister* and *angel* and the *devil*. The Britons kept their own language which the Saxons called Welsh (it means foreign), and still today, the Welsh with true British persistency, go on talking British. But the Gaelic group of languages that occupied our islands before the Saxons (Welsh, Cornish, Gaelic, Erse) have had hardly any influence on English and what they have had has been only the addition of single words, not change of structure. *Whiskey* is their leading contribution to our speech.

.    .    .    .    .    .    .

The partial conquest of England by the Danes and the occupation of the North had a more real effect on the language by blending it with a cognate tongue. The blend was a peculiar one. The languages were so closely alike that Danish words, even pronouns, could slip into English on their merits. *They, their,* and *them* are Danish; so too very many common words, elementary words such as *sky* and *skull* and *wing*, etc. Strangely enough the verb *die* is Danish. The Saxons couldn't die in three letters; so the snappy Danish word beat out the Saxon which degenerated into our *starve*. The Danes spread over the country (they ruled two thirds of it) a lot of place-names, ending in *by* (*Whitby*) and *dale*, and *thorpe*, etc. The greatest change came from the Norman Conquest. Even before

1066 the court of the Saxon King, Edward the Confessor, was filled with Frenchmen, and French was acquiring its peculiar status as a polite language which it still kept in the Victorian drawing rooms and the diplomatic intercourse of yesterday. It is odd how long English carried the opprobrium of its lowly origin and French the affectation of its excellence.

There were about two million English in England in 1066. Not enough Normans ever came over to teach them French. Nor did the Normans want to, nor contrariwise. French was the language of the court, not the castle; Latin of the Church and the government, English of the people. For obvious reasons the situation gradually changed; of necessity and by force of numbers and circumstances the English language worked its way up. No one, so far as I know, has ever traced in full the vanishing of French. It seems settled that for nearly 200 years it kept its isolated superiority. But its hold was shaken by the tyranny of King John, which jumbled the people together, and utterly lost by the long wars (the Hundred Years' War) with France (1338-1453). It is understood that by 1350 all people whose children enjoyed the benefit of school teaching wanted their children taught in English. Then came men of genius—a genius for language—such as notably Geoffrey Chaucer (1340-1400) and showed how English could be cultivated and elevated and refashioned into a wonderful medium of writing. A little later the Tudor and Elizabethan writers carried the process further, until we reach the plays of Shakespeare and the English of King James's Bible—an English practically our own.

But English, when it thus came back, was like Dido's husband when a ghost, greatly changed from its former self. Its elaborate old endings and suffixes were all gone or going. Very few have survived. An Anglo-Saxon primer shows us nouns with separate endings for separate cases, numbers and genders, as in German today. Not only did the noun carry a string of needless variations but the articles and the adjectives shared them. In English we say "the good, old red wine" and that's the whole of it. But in Anglo-Saxon, as in German today, they had half a dozen ways of saying it. They named it in the nominative and drank it in the accusative, joined it up with suffixes that coupled it up like a train of box cars. The sheer waste of human effort involved can only be compared to the still more appalling waste of our English spelling, and would be about as hard to terminate—that is, nominally very simple, practically just about impossible. If the Germans have the good luck to be as completely conquered as the Saxons were they may have their language improved for them in the same way as with Saxon English.

For the conquerors who presently took over English speech never learned to distinguish its elaborate suffixes, except a few of the simple ones. To them good, old, red wine was good, old red wine. There were a few outstanding survivals such as our use of 's for a possessive case—*John's* hat. Even that can be replaced by "of"—*the reign of John*. There is also the use of *s* or *es* to indicate the plural to which practically all English words are now assimilated. There survive a few old plurals in *n*—*oxen, children*—some of them almost

vanished—*hosen, shoon*—or plurals from the old Anglo-Saxon made by changing the vowels in the word as
when *mouse* becomes *mice,* or with both the vowel
change and the final *n,* as in *kine* and *brethren.* Gone
also, and this is a specially good riddance, are the confused primitive genders that persist in French and German and most European languages whereby a whole
mass of inanimate things are male and female, with
masculine and feminine adjectives to "agree" with
them. In French a bicycle is *she,* in German a girl is *it;*
in some European languages (French) an army is *she,*
in others *it,* and in others *he.* All this useless muddle
of meaningless form comes down to us as a survival
of primitive thought which animated all things, saw a
spirit in fire and a demon in smoke.

These gender forms broke down in the remaking
of Saxon into English and left us with no other distinction than that of male and female, animate or lifeless
—*he, she* and *it,* with the plurals all lumped as *they.*
The use of the neuter *it* spreads commonly over all the
animate world of plants, and at will, over animals—a
horse is *he* or *it.*

An odd anomaly exists in modern English whereby
we talk of all ships and vessels as *she.* This is not a
legacy of Saxon or Danish times. It is easy to see that
it connects with the idea of a vessel as a thing of life
and movement. But even at that, why not *he?* How
strange it would seem to English people, how natural
to French people, to search the horizon for an approaching ship, and say, "I see him; there he is." This
feminine gender for ships spread with the machine age
to all kinds of engines and machines. A locomotive is

"she" to *her* engineer. Even a lawn-mower is *she* to the mechanic who "oils *her* up good."

Fancy may renew, and poetry may revive the gender forms, as when the violet droops her head, or the sun shoots his angry beams. But this is only in connection with the make-believe of personification, and adds a power to English not known to a language like French where the violet is always *she* even when sold in a bunch, and the sun is always *he,* whether angry or astronomical.

Casting out its worn-out and valueless suffixes, the English language developed in their stead an extensive use of prepositions to indicate relations between things. These also came to be used to modify the meaning of a verb, in such a way that a simple root from *take* or *do* or *break* could enter into a large number of combinations with varying shades of meaning. Think of all that we can do with *break* by combining it with prepositions used in this adverbial way. *Thieves break in. Fire breaks out. A meeting breaks up when a speaker breaks down and has to break off.* All languages possess this faculty in some degree but English is pre-eminent.

This great development came to us by the mingling of Norman French with English, or rather by submerging Norman French into the plastic base of English that lay below it. But the process was carried further when the revival of learning brought a new infusion of Latin, and presently of Greek forms, into the English language, quite apart from the Latin element that had been brought by the Church, or had come indirectly with the French language and the forms of

law. A countless number of words, those of a rounded
dignity and evenness of syllables, were thus dragged
over bodily from the Latin, like the prisoners in the
children's game of prisoner's base—as when *we indicate subordinate positions for extinct animals*—
Their number is legion. With them, with more inertia,
as if reluctantly, came the Greek forms, or Greek that
had passed through Latin, when a *philanthropic phi-
losopher apologizes for megalomania.*

·   ·   ·   ·   ·   ·   ·

This means that our English language has several
layers of words like buried geological strata. Deep
down are the good old Anglo-Saxon words for the
simple objects, the first things, the plain sights and
sounds of life—*father, mother* and *children, house* and
*home* and *hearth,* the *dawn,* the *day,* the *dusk,* the
*night,* the *end.* In any example of beautiful and simple
language, poetry or prose, that deals with beautiful
and simple things these old root words of English will
be found to predominate.

> *The curfew tolls the knell of parting day,*
> *The lowing herd winds slowly o'er the lea,*
> *The ploughman homeward plods his weary way.*

> *A little slumber, a little sleep, a little*
> *Folding of the hands to sleep . . .*

·   ·   ·   ·   ·   ·   ·

But deep down in this layer lie also certain old Norman French words, like *curfew* itself (cover-fire), so
early in the language, so long embedded in it and so
rounded to its form that they are almost part of it.

Here belong a lot of Norman French terms like *pork* and *mutton* and *beef* and *venison,* that carry down the stamp of the conquest. The good things eaten and used by the masters appear in the French tongue of the *cuisine.* The animals killed for it keep the Saxon barnyard and forest names—sheep and ox and deer. The Norman touch is on *sauce* and *jelly* and the *feast.* Plain *breakfast* to stave off hunger is Saxon.

Next above these are a lot of French terms that recall the days of *castles* and *tournaments* and *chivalry,* of *heralds* and *tapestry,* such as these words themselves. Many of these were never really at home, never passed into the English language, and survive only in the uses of the Heralds' College, or in poetry that at times uses them as embellishment—words like *joust,* and *gules.* Above this came the full ponderous weight of the imported book Latin, continually deposited like a stratum of iron ore lying over what was once flowers. With that is intermingled here and there the still heavier metal of Greek as taken over by the Renaissance scholars and divines. It is amazing to what an extent this infiltration of Latin and Greek terms in one form and another had made English not merely a new language but in a sense a double language, retaining the old forms beside the new. By the time of the Reformation it was possible to write whole sentences of learned English without an English word; to say, for example: *Pontifical prelates fulminate anathemas denouncing heretical doctrines.* This has come a long way from *Holy men chide wicked words.*

.    .    .    .    .    .    .    .    .

With such changes we reach the full beauty of the English of the Elizabethans and of the Stuart time. The English of Shakespeare blends the Saxon and the classical forms, the Saxon for mystic and picturesque effect, the classical for greater exactitude. Hamlet's *Soliloquy* shows the balance in the forms as below, with classical words italicized:

To be or not to be, that is the *question;*
Whether 'tis *nobler* in the mind to *suffer*
The slings and arrows of *outrageous fortune,*
Or to take *arms* against a sea of troubles,
And by *opposing* end them . . . . . . .
. . . . . . . . . . . . . . . To die,—to sleep;—
To sleep! *perchance* to dream—ay, there's the rub;
For in that sleep of death what dreams may come
When we have shuffled off this *mortal coil,*
. . . . . . . . . . . . There's the *respect*
That makes *calamity* of so long life;

    .     .     .     .     .     .     .

Nor does the development of our language, at least on the side of its vocabulary, end at this point of our history. The expansion of British Commerce and Settlement overseas brought with it a wealth of foreign terms that were picked up and assimilated all round the globe:—Here is *tea* (it should be *tay*) from China, *coffee* (it means the drink) from Arabia, *muslin* from the Moslem countries and *macaroni* from Italy. The North American Indians contributed *moccasins* and *tomahawks*. Mexico sent over *tomatoes* and *chocolate*. Our words are drawn from all over the world. A hussar in *mufti* in a *harem* in a *jungle* eating *paprika* with a *dervish* is covering about three million square miles.

A further expansion of the language was made possible by the growth of popular literature, the popular press and the novel. Rural dialect and metropolitan speech were stirred and mingled. There was a fermentation from below, the speech of Mrs. Gamp and Mr. Weller sending out its challenge to Oxford. Slang and jargon moved up into respectability, while in America slang has represented something like a rebirth of language or at least a revival of its vital principle. Yet at the same time the progress of modern science and medicine and their perpetual demand for Greek to name things yet unnamed, serve as a steadying influence, a connecting link with the past, a brake on the wheels of change. This is seen every time that a *lounge-lizard* uses a *telephone*.

    .    .    .    .    .    .    .

There can be no doubt that the English language, thus developed, has attained a width and wealth of vocabulary, a power of expression superior to those of any other languages, old or new. Anyone who would write English should cultivate an appreciation amounting almost to affection for its wonderful vocabulary. Children are often set to write exercises in words of one syllable. It would be an excellent thing to set authors to do the same. They would learn to appreciate afresh the wonderful range of our language, its wealth of synonyms that enable us to set aside many of our oldest words as too good for daily use.

    .    .    .    .    .    .    .

The appreciation of words is one thing, over-appreciation is another. Just as negroes are said to be fond of big words for their own sake (*How do yo' symptoms seem to segastulate?*), so there have always been people over-fascinated with the art of words. This has always led to fantastic, over-fine writing and speech, to the use of words for words' sake, to round-about ways of expressing a straight idea. One recalls historically the affectations current in Molière's day in French aristocratic circles whose speech is satirized in the play *Les Précieuses Ridicules,* where would-be fashionable ladies, not wishing to call a chair by such a plain name as a chair, call it a *commodity for conversation.* In all ages pompous people use a pompous language, half-educated people an over-educated speech, and people of small intellect run to words a size too large. The search for novelty joins with the vanity of self-expression to produce new and worthless forms.

Now this was never more true than it is today. It happens that we need a lot of new words because we live among a lot of new things. Aviators *zip* and *zoom* and *nose-dive* in and out of *hangars* and over *aerodromes, bank* and *stall* and *tail-spin,* till language can hardly keep up with them or fall so fast. These words for the most part are so new and so different that there is no quarrel with them. But the motor-car, which is after all only a first cousin to a horse, now presumes to take old words and squeezes them into new ones. Has a garage man the right to offer to *service* you— as a valet once served you? The march of invention, the processes of crime and pursuit, the devastation of war, overwhelm us in a rush of new words . . . *barrages, smoke-screen, camouflage,* so that even the first World War is antiquated and we must have today *um-*

*brellas* of fire, *pill-boxes* of defense and the huge word *Maginot*—huge in significance, stranded in the language like a dead whale to indicate a degree of ineptitude never named before.

Nor was there ever a time of greater facility in making new words. We can still fall back on the old-time process of using old Greek as new English. The process that gave the nineteenth century the *telegraph* and the *telephone* and the *phonograph* . . . is still alive in the twentieth. But more than this we have kept alive, indeed more alive than ever, the power to make new compounds—*die-hards, hold-ups, work-outs,* etc. It is especially in America that this renewed vitality of language is apparent. Indeed, we seem to prefer on this continent new, expressive compounds that convey a physical image to words whose earlier colour has faded. A robber is a *gun-man,* and a failure is a *wash-out.* All this is very well but the danger is that we are apt to be huddled forward into all sorts of new expressions of no particular value and merely representing a second name for something well-named already. Why should we use *motivate* when we have *actuate* already? If Mr. Smith, who is reported in the day's news as having beaten up his wife, is *actuated* by jealousy, why not say so instead of *motivating* him? A great many of our new verbalisms are due to the present-day passion for all that goes under the name of psychology, presenting a glimpse, as it were, into the inner relations of this. Hence, such words as *prospect* to replace the older *customer* and *client,* and the awful word *contact* which replaces good old phrases such as *to get hold of* or *get in touch with.* These two were really excellent. If you *get hold of* a man—by a button—you have him at your disposal for conversation. To *contact* him sounds like sniffing around him. But *contact* has just that psychological over-sharpness about it which seems to appeal. Hence, an up-to-date business firm would not instruct a representative in old fashioned terms to *go and see* Mr. Jones. That's not done. You must *approach* Mr. Jones, then *contact* him, then try out his *reaction*—and then you give him a cigar and he says "Yes," just as he would have anyway. Modern business and modern advertising throws forward a whole barrage of language in its advance.

Nor is it only business that gets verbose. Official business, in a day when official bodies have multiplied tenfold, runs to "official" language, meaning language that says a simple thing in complex form for the sake of imagined dignity. The London *Times,* discussing not long ago this tendency, quotes as authentic a superb example of this "ribbon writing." A British diplomatic document tried to express the idea that all the people present at a conference strongly favoured international peace. It did so in the following terms:

*The unity of view of the participants in the conversations has been established regarding the exceptional importance at the present time of an all-embracing collective organization of security on the basis of the indivisibility of peace.*

The text is quoted by Mr. A. P. Herbert (*What A Word, 1935*), who has devoted all the power of his outstanding humour and satire to denunciation of this "jungle" English. Among other phrases culled by Mr. Herbert from magazines, journals of good standing we find . . . *In motoring, the personal factor of the driver plays a preponderating part.* The old, bad English for this used to be, *The driver is what counts.* Burns could have greatly improved on his *A man's a man for a' that,* if he had known enough to write . . . *The preponderating part of a man is the man's own preponderation.*

Here is another example: *Are we quite sure,* asks a modern review, *whether the newly-emancipated woman has secured for herself a harmonious psycho-physiological equilibrium?* This seems to me to recall the old bar-room test of sobriety—Can she walk along a chalk line, or will she fall over? Here is a telephone announcement: *Residents not wishing at the time to take a call can have their presence negatived by the operator.*

But this use of overdone language must not be held to condemn all attempts to polish, improve and revise. To state the case idiomatically in our flexible language, we may say that the fact that language can be overdone need not prevent us from doing it over. The practise of writers varies very much in this aspect. All students have read how Shakespeare's printers claimed that he "never blotted a line." Of this statement as much has been made, and made as ineptly, as of most of the few little authentic fragments of information about the man who wrote the plays of Shakespeare. The statement of itself means nothing. Shakespeare may have made a fair copy, or hired someone else to make it. Those of us who write books now do not blot lines either; the publishers see to it that we don't.

But among modern authors we read of the scrupulous care of Robert Louis Stevenson, of his writing and re-writing, polishing and improving, as an optician perfects a glass; and of the hand-picked phrases of Walter Pater, the British essayist; and of the repeated revisions of Goldwin Smith. To people fascinated with perfection such revision seems craftsmanship, as opposed to the slap-dash ease of a writer trailing ink across a page as a house-painter trails whitewash. To other minds it seems as if the first fine careless rapture were everything; as if the thought and the words must be conceived together and fused in a white heat of creation; as if this later tinkering with cold metal could only deface the original beauty of the cast. There is no doubt truth both ways; there always is, over anything worth talking about. A certain revision there must be, if only to put in the commas and verify the spelling. Such revision is certain to find a poor word here, a clumsy phrase there or accidental repetitions easy to correct when seen. But there is always the danger of substituting for what was bad something that is worse, of making dullness duller by expanding it and obscurity obscurer by adding a light that fails. There is always a danger that a style too carefully pruned and revised may begin to look as artificial as an overclipped tree; that the midnight oil burned on revision may leave on the page the smell of the lamp.

Much must depend on the individual. Some people in writing can retain a firm grasp on the original idea while altering its first expression. Others can't. They begin to write something else.

Much depends also on the kind of thing that is being written—a poem, a story, an essay, a history, an epitaph, a joke. Poetry supposedly comes straight from the poet's throat; in reality much of it, of necessity, out of the rhyme book, whether the rhyme book is in print or a register in the poet's head. Hence, while nominally all inspiration, poetry of the common sort is ninety per cent revision after the start. At its highest reach thought and words and rhyme all come together.

But there are other fields. One would imagine that historical writing and essay writing lend themselves to revision, and even demand it, far more than story writing in which so much depends on the "first shot." At the tail end of the list humour lends itself least to revision and depends most on the happy first thought. Fun in words is as hard to recapture as a laugh is hard to repeat.

# CHAPTER IV

## THE COMPLETE THOUGHT CALLED A SENTENCE

*The melody of prose — The short sentence — Its merits and its defects — The guilty language of lawyers; afraid to stop — The tanglefoot sentence — George Washington who, when whatever . . . etc. — Paragraphs and the printer's need of make-up — Without it even Dante's "Inferno" would look like Hell — The old blue laws of the paragraph — The paragraphs of the Plains of Abraham*

WITH that we turn from words to sentences. Now sentence-making is a wonderful art. For people of literary sensibility (you and me) every piece of prose, whether history or essay or fiction or conversation or argument, runs as a sort of tune, with not only the rhythm of the single words or phrases, but the march and time of the whole. The long rolling sentences of Gibbon or Macaulay sweep along like the waves on the Channel beaches. The short sentences of the Scripture beat like the clock of time. A brilliant essayist suggests the warmth of a steady fire, at times crackling into explosions. A Scottish historical novel moves through its drowsy introduction till it lulls us asleep in the heather. A modern Edgar Wallace page is as broken as the pistol shots that punctuate it. . . . All of this effect arises from the distinctive run of the sentences.

The making of clear and beautiful sentences in harmony with the movement of thought is a high art. It demands a native sensitiveness to word-values and with it a long practice. A French barber once told me—standing off a little for a preliminary view of me—that to him every customer was a new problem. We may not be able to reach up to that but we can see that, for people who write, every sentence matters, and still more the run and movement of the prose written.

. . . . . . .

Most of us have learned from a little school manual that a complete thought put into words is called a sentence. But the difficulty is to know when the thought *is* complete, and whether it needs a few trimmings and qualifications in the form of subordinate clauses. These are themselves really sentences or would be so, if they stood alone. If we said all that we had to say in the form of single sentences it would sound as simple as Simple Simon.

Thus no one would say or write:

*John Smith is my neighbour. I am on very good terms with him. We went to school together. Therefore, I often go fishing with him. I hope to go tomorrow. John may be free. John may not be free.*

We would rather say:

*I hope to go fishing tomorrow with John Smith with whom I often go fishing as he is my neighbour and I am on very good terms with him as we were at school together.*

We have only to take one or two practical examples to realize how difficult and how needless it would be to write our ordinary stories in consecutive single sentences. Here is the opening sentence of that famous old book, Charles Kingsley's *Westward Ho:*—

*All who have travelled through the delicious scenery of North Devon, must needs know the little white town of Bideford, which slopes upwards from its broad tide-river paved with yellow sands, and many-arched old bridge where salmon wait for autumn floods, towards the pleasant upland on the west.*

Here it is changed into single sentences:

*People have travelled through the delicious scenery of North Devon. All these people must needs know the little white town of Bideford. This slopes upwards from its broad tide-river with yellow sands and many-arched old bridge towards the pleasant uplands on the west. Salmon wait at this bridge for autumn floods.*

Pretty good but not exactly the same thing. Try this. Here is the opening sentence of one of Mr. Freeman Wills Croft's magical crime stories:

*No one would have thought from Anne Day's appearance as she sat with closed eyes in the corner of her third-class carriage, that her mind was seething with a delicious excitement.*

Transposed it runs:

*Anne Day sat with closed eyes in the corner of her third-class carriage. Her mind was seething with a de-*

*licious excitement. No one would have thought thus from Anne Day's appearance.*

Pretty good; but too slow for crime. At that rate Anne Day would never get murdered—perhaps she didn't anyway. I forget.

. . . . . . .

But in some cases the attempt to turn things into single sentences would be just about hopeless, if not comic. What are we to say of this, the opening of Boswell's *Life of Johnson?*

*To write the life of him who excelled all mankind in writing the lives of others and who, whether we consider his extraordinary endowments or his various works, has been equalled by few in any age is an arduous and may be reckoned in me a presumptuous task.*

The trouble here is that we don't know where to get at it. It is like trying to catch a hen. Obviously the main statement is that something is an arduous task, but we have got to go back to find it. It will turn into something like this:

*Dr. Johnson excelled all mankind in writing the lives of others. Consider his extraordinary endowments. Now consider his various works. He has been equalled by few in any age. To write his life is an arduous task. It may be reckoned in me a presumptuous task.*

This is about as close to Japanese prose—if we put *humble worm* for *me*—as one would wish to go. But in English it won't stand.

. . . . . . .

In other words we very soon reach the conclusion that sentences which are to correspond to our form of thinking have got to be qualified by the inclusion of subordinate and conditional ideas. Rodin's *Thinker* might take his thoughts one by one, but we can't.

In spite of this, however, the principal thing which I would wish to emphasize in this connection, the main precept I wish to inculcate, is a warning against long and complicated and qualified sentences, and a plea for short and direct ones.

Let it be said at once that some sentences are long only in appearance. The connecting words are mere couplings. The sentences stand alone.

Witness this passage that after more than a hundred and sixty years still thrills the American heart:

*These are the times that try men's souls. The summer soldier and the sunshine patriot will in this crisis shrink from the service of his country; but he that stands it now deserves the thanks of man and woman. Tyranny, like hell, is not easily conquered; yet we have this consolation with us, that the harder the conflict the more glorious the triumph. What we obtain too cheap we esteem too lightly; 'tis dearness alone that gives everything its value.*

Or take a characteristic descriptive passage by Charles Dickens, the kind which he loved to use as the opening of a novel. In the mere form of printing the sentences seem endless. But in the sense of their meaning they consist of a series of short statements.

*London. Michaelmas Term lately over, and the Lord Chancellor sitting in Lincoln's Inn Hall. Im-*

*placable November weather. . . . Fog everywhere.*
*Fog up the river, where it flows among green aits*
*(islets) and meadows; fog down the river, where it*
*rolls defiled among the tiers of shipping, and the water-*
*side pollutions of a great (and dirty) city. Fog on the*
*Essex marshes, fog on the Kentish heights. Fog creep-*
*ing into the cabooses of collier-brigs; fog lying out on*
*the yards, and hovering in the rigging of great ships;*
*fog drooping on the gunwales of barges and small*
*boats. etc. . . .*

Legal sentences must of necessity be long. A lawyer
dare not stop. If he ever seems to have brought a thing
to a complete end then somebody may discover something left unsaid and invalidate everything. The Tenth
Commandment is able to say *Thou shalt not steal.* A
lawyer has to say: *Subject always to the provisions of*
*clauses 8-20 below thou shall not steal except as here-*
*inafter provided.* Even at that the lawyer would have
to take another look at the word *steal,* and scratch it
out in favour of *Thou shall not steal, pilfer, rob, ap-*
*propriate, hook, swipe, or in any other way obtain un-*
*lawful possession of anything.* Then the word *thing*
would start him off again to write *thing, object, com-*
*modity, chattel, property . . .*

．　　　．　　　．　　　．　　　．　　　．　　　．

Now this inhibition that prevents the lawyer from
stopping at the end of a sentence lies in a certain measure on all who write. In ever so many ordinary cases
the qualification of what is said has practically got to
be said in the same sentence. Otherwise we seem to
have first said something and then unsaid it. We write

*You mustn't go down to the end of the town unless you go down with me.*

That seems without doubt a necessity of thought with us. Oddly enough the Greeks didn't find it so. A Greek could write, ask Xenophon if he couldn't:

*Now there was no grass in all this desert. If there was any it was very short.*

Similarly a Greek could write:

*Not a drum was heard, not a funeral note. A few drums were beating uptown.*

.    .    .    .    .    .    .

To a certain extent qualifying clauses are perfectly natural and help to show the balance of what is important and what is secondary. Thus Fielding writes in his *Tom Jones:*

*It was Mr. Weston's custom every afternoon, as soon as he was drunk, to hear his daughter play on the harpsichord.*

The emphasis is on the harpsichord; the *drunk* is neither here nor there, except to indicate the time.

.    .    .    .    .    .    .

We may grant of course the literary value of long and beautiful sentences written into the prose of narrative, or the long yet balanced sentences of essay and argument. We may grant also the value of long sentences varied and broken with short ones. A specially striking effect is obtained when a short sentence, a sort of announcement introduces and indicates the matter that follows:

*The blow was soon to fall. In the dead of night in the glare and tumult of a summer thunderstorm, two hundred ferocious Iroquois broke over the unhappy village . . . etc.*

If you look into the pages of any author whose style is worth considering you will find such effects used to their full advantage. The sentences, as was said at the outset, fall into a sort of rhythm specially designed to fit the sense.

. . . . . . .

But all said and done we may still repeat, beware of the qualifying clause. With many writers, the everlasting use of qualifying matter, in things other than fiction, arises largely from a fear of inaccuracy, a dread of contradiction and disproof that makes them afraid to state a plain fact. Nothing, indeed, is absolutely true. The earth is not quite round. The sky is not quite blue. Rain isn't altogether wet. Hence any statement that you can make has some kind of limitation to it. Writers who are obsessed with limitations, exceptions and approximations become unable to say a thing straight out and let it alone. They never say that a thing is, they say that it may be said to be. They don't say that a thing never happens; they say that it virtually never happens; they don't say that Old Grimes is dead; they say that he is as good as dead, or is dead for all practical purposes, in other words may be said to be virtually dead. They might go so far as to say that he is as dead as a doornail.

. . . . . . .

Very many academic writers, and many professors in their classroom lectures develop this peculiar hesitation. Many of us in our college days listened to such talk as:

*. . . and now, gentlemen, we come to the so-called French Revolution, culminating in the so-called Reign of Terror and occasioning the so-called Great War which spread around the so-called world.*

In a somewhat similar way writers, including writers of eminence, are misled into the over-use of subordinate sentences by trying to pack too much into too little. In their overpacked sentences the meaning has not room to turn round. They are packed as a woman packs a valise, a mosaic never to be re-set, as compared with the easy, open spaces left by a man.

.  .  .  .  .  .  .

Most objectionable of all are sentences made with subordinate clauses introduced by relative pronouns and conjunctions that are telescoped in together one after the other, each clause modifying the one in front of it. It is a peculiarity of our English construction that we can actually begin a sentence:

*London which, when, what . . .*

or:

*Edward who, whatever, where . . .*

and still manage to get away with it. Thus, to make a full sentence of this type.

*George Washington who, when whatever he attempted had failed, never despaired.*

It is not often that authors perplex their prose with three of these things. But the use of two is very common and indeed becomes a mannerism. Nor is it only in the negative sense, as avoiding confusion, that short sentences come into their own. There is a great power in them, in their very finality. In good narration, what we call breathless narration, the short sentences, one following the other, are like the stages of the action itself. Even if of necessity a little broken and joined here and there by plain coupling words (*and*—*but*—etc. etc.), the short sentences, though no longer short in the sense of punctuation, are short in their essential bearing.

Here is Huckleberry Finn, making his escape from the cabin beside the river where his "pop" had locked him in:

*I took the sack of corn meal and took it to where the canoe was hid and shoved the vines and branches apart and put it in; then I done the same with the side of bacon; then the whiskey-jug; I took all the coffee and sugar there was and all the ammunition; I took the wadding; I took the bucket and gourd; took a tin dipper and a cup, and the skillet and the coffee-pot. I took fish lines and matches and other things. I cleaned out the place.*

. . . . . . .

In the old-fashioned books on rhetoric much was made of the formation of paragraphs. Indeed the Scottish writers, who loved severity, took the paragraph in custody under a set of rules called the Laws of the

Paragraph. But little need be made of this now. In the printer's sense a paragraph is becoming not a break in the sense, but a break in the type. It is made as a gardener trims a border with a hoe, knocking a little gap wherever it looks pretty. It is part of the new need for "make-up" that goes with our magazines and newspapers of today. Even our books share it. From a printer's point of view it doesn't so much matter what is *in* a book as what is outside of it; what is *in* a chapter as what is over it; and what is *on* a page so much as what is round a page. In the brute commercial sense there is a good deal in this. People are attracted to neat pages, artistically broken into trim sections. Set a thing into solid unending blocks of type, into pages that never break and few books could get over. Milton's *Paradise* would be lost and Dante's *Inferno* would look like Hell.

The paragraph, therefore, in the sense of a division of type is vanishing. It remains as a division of the sense—a pause in a story, an opening of an argument. But it is doubtful if we can with any advantage reduce this to law. A paragraph is in reality a consequence not a cause. You don't make a paragraph; you merely, as it were, run out of breath. Now no one would plan his breathing for his exercise; he takes his exercise and his breathing must take the consequence.

The older notion was that written language naturally ran, as it were, in successive waves. The form of movement of these could be guided, and their advance indicated. Thus Law No. 1 of the Paragraph, as quoted from a bygone manual:

*The opening sentence of the paragraph, unless obviously introductory, must indicate with clearness the subject of the paragraph.*

This is excellent—sometimes—a lot of times. But there is no law about it. Very often the effect was very happy as carried out by authors of the past generation who aimed deliberately at a formal style. Francis Parkman is a good example. Open his *Wolfe and Montcalm* and you will find, with no attempt at search, these paragraph openings used with evident effect.

Here are the chief paragraph headings with which Wolfe wins the Battle of the Plains of Abraham:

*For full two hours the procession of boats, borne on the current, steered silently down the St. Lawrence.*

*The main body of troops waited in their boats by the edge of the strand.*

*Before many of them had reached the top, cannon were heard close on the left.*

*The day broke in clouds and threatening rain.*

*Montcalm had passed a troubled night.*

*Montcalm was amazed at what he saw.*

*Montcalm and his chief officers held a council of war.*

*The English waited the result with a composure which, if not real, was at least well-feigned.*

*Wolfe was everywhere.*

*Montcalm, still on horseback, was borne with the tide of fugitives towards the town.*

There are other paragraphs as well but with headings less pointed. A Scottish rhetoric expert might have claimed that Wolfe should have had a paragraph all to himself to die in. In place of that, his death comes in the two page paragraph of the climax of the battle. Apart from this the chapter is a fine example of this style of writing at its best.

But all that can be said for this formal structure of paragraphs is that it is one good way to write. Another good way is to wander, to seem to drift in a kind of discursive style that is willing to make digressions and, if need be, to get nowhere. Under the "laws" of the paragraph no digression could be made except as a paragraph itself, duly marked with a sign—like the BUMP sign on a highway.

. . . . . . .

Indeed, all the laws of the paragraph ran to this same artificiality and monotonous regularity. Thus the second law concerned the use of the "connective" words that must link the sentences together so that the bearing of each upon what had preceded must be plain and unmistakable. At least two generations of British and American writers were badly damaged by this law. I recall an old professor who began every fourth sentence with *Hence accordingly*. That meant, here's a new start, boys. It was followed in regular order by *of course, therefore, however*. It sounded like this:

*Hence accordingly* Julius Caesar invaded Britain. The Britons, *of course,* determined to oppose him. They *therefore* defended the beaches. The Romans *however* easily overcame their resistance. *Hence accordingly* Caesar marched to London, etc.

    •     •     •     •     •     •     •

Take it all in all I do not think that forming paragraphs is part of the art of writing. It is putting the cart before the horse. Good writing, one kind of good writing, results in measured paragraphs just as painting a portrait results in a distribution of paint. Painters, I admit, talk of a "composition" but I should imagine that the picture comes first and the paint afterwards.

## CHAPTER V

## THE ART OF NARRATION

*Never mind the plot — There are only three anyway — It's all in the telling — Find the right word — Keep off worn-out phrases — The boy stood on the burning deck until his whereabouts became a matter of speculation — Metaphors straight and mixed — Watering a spark to make it a mustard tree. The narrator of the story: Omniscience? Or do I tell it: or do they tell it in letters? Romance and realism — Fancy or photograph — The art of description — Don't keep a murder waiting — Prosy prose*

Most people, especially those who have never thought about it, would be apt to suppose that a story depends chiefly on a plot, and that story-telling—the art of narration—consists chiefly on finding or inventing an interesting plot. We speak of stories as having "a wonderful plot." In a well-developed story the plot is supposed to thicken and to brew till it boils over in a climax. One thinks of the hundred and one stories of that fertile and facile genius, the late Edgar Wallace. They seem all plot and nothing else, and they gather momentum like a cyclone till they reach a sort of waterspout climax in which criminals and detectives chase one another in circles in aeroplanes, disappear, crawl out of sewers and grapple again.

In other words the plot is supposed to tangle and

then slowly untangle, until it turns out in the end that almost everybody is somebody else. In other stories again the plot deepens and darkens and gets so mysterious that the reader loses it altogether. This was especially the case with the books of Charles Dickens. The plot, as in *Little Dorrit,* got so unfathomable that at last the readers leave it to Dickens himself and are content with just the characters. Many of Dickens's plots, indeed, are too complicated for comprehension or too preposterous for belief. People crawl round in their disguises for years, acting a part or leading a double life, in order to find out and divulge the fact that somebody was someone else—thirty years ago. But the most celebrated of Dickens's books, the *Pickwick Papers,* had no plot or none at the start, except that Mr. Pickwick and his associates were commissioned by the Pickwick Club to travel as long as they liked and as far as they liked, provided that they did it at their own expense.

Now if Charles Dickens was the greatest writer of fiction who ever lived, as some of us think he was, then this aspect of his work merits attention. It means that, after all, plot can't be everything, and in fact the more you look into it the less and less important plot will seem as compared with the other elements that enter into story-telling. Many people who would like to write get the idea that if they could only "think of a good plot," the thing would be done. To which the answer is, My dear sir, if you thought of the best plot in the world you wouldn't be any nearer to it. A *plot* only means that certain things happen to certain characters in certain places. But unless you can make the characters live and the place rise before the eye and make the incidents really happen—all of which is part of the art of narration—the mere statement that they did happen won't interest anybody. That is why so many of our current mystery and crime stories fail to raise a shudder or start a thrill. If Mr. X., who is nothing more than just Mr. X., as lifeless as a dead letter, is found dead by Messrs. Y. and Z., in an apartment on Q. street, we are frankly, like Queen Victoria, not amused. The characters are as dead as the corpse and are all one to us.

Not long ago an anonymous writer in *Punch* beautifully illustrated this idea in a burlesque detective story. He speaks of the finding of the body and of how, at the sight of it, Detective Trumper, "accustomed as he was to scenes of horror, could scarcely *suppress a yawn.*" This is beautiful, not only as an exquisite example of the technique of humour but also in showing the power of humour to reveal a hidden truth. Why did Trumper yawn? Well, don't you see, why shouldn't he? The body was of no particular interest. Trumper must have felt with the poet, *'Tis but another dead, all you say is said.* They're killing bookfuls every year.

．　　．　　．　　．　　．　　．　　．

What we are saying then is that a plot as reduced to a statement is just a frame. The work is still to do. For any writers who are looking for plots, here are some good ones, so good that they were used thousands, or hundreds of years ago:—

One. A man goes down to hell to get his wife. He

plays the lyre so well that the devil lets her go. Later he's sorry. Hundreds of poets worked on this.

Two. A man goes down to hell, as a visitor, meets a lot of old acquaintances and comes up again. Dante made a great hit with this.

Three. A man sells his soul to the devil, has a good time, and finds there's nothing in it. Goethe thrilled all the world with this.

These are famous plots, which belong to the history of the world's literature. Yet in and of themselves they don't seem hard to think of. Any married man might dream the first; any sociable old fellow the second; and the third is what many students have tried at college.

Nor do the plots of world famous books of the present epoch seem much harder to invent than the classical ones.

Here is one of today:

*An old man has taught in a school for forty years. And then dies over tea and toast.*

Here is one of yesterday:

*A girl who is not married has a baby and kills it and is hanged.*

Indeed, any student of literature can easily realize the difference between being told a plot in outline and reading its actual conversion into a story. Even anyone who is not a student of literature can realize it the next time any of his friends, thrilled with a new thriller, undertakes to tell him what it is about.

To show, in a didactic way, this relation as between the plot of a story and the telling of a story, let us take a practical illustration. Here we have a world famous story, the *Strange Case of Dr. Jekyll and Mr. Hyde* by Robert Louis Stevenson, which at first sight seems to typify the preëminence of plot. Yet if we start from the mere outline and try to tell the story, we soon find in what class we belong.

.     .     .     .     .     .     .

Dr. Henry Jekyll is a London physician of wealth and reputation, a handsome, genial man, as wholesome to the eye as is his apparent personality to the mind. But there is concealed in him a desire for dissipation, for a double life. He would like to be "tough" if he had the opportunity. Chance gives it to him. The accidental discovery of a medicinal powder enables him to transform his appearance. His body seems to shrink, his face to distort, his limbs to *shrivel*. At will, he can convert himself to a "double," and an infamous creature, Edward Hyde, revelling in sin, takes the temporary place of Henry Jekyll. The inevitable follows. Evil multiplies. Hyde is led to crime—to murder. Henry Jekyll, stricken with shivering horror and repentance, finds the operation of the drug has gone beyond his power. Locked in his surgery, as Hyde, unable to re-escape into himself, his agonies of mind end in suicide.

.     .     .     .     .     .     .

As the story draws towards its end its underlying meaning, never explicitly set forth, seems to grow luminous beneath the printed page. It reveals that strange duality of good and evil that is in us all.

.     .     .     .     .     .     .

Very good. Now try to write that out in 20,000 words. You can't. You don't know how to begin. Start

with Henry Jekyll as a boy at school? You'll get prosy
and wander all over the place. The reader will never
get beyond matriculation. Start with the news of the
murder done by Edward Hyde, as cried in the streets
and posted in headlines? Quite so, you'll get excitement for five minutes and just settle down into the old
stuff of Inspector Higginbottom, making notes, and
picking up clues, and Hector Trumper suppressing a
yawn and the arrival of the Great Detective with a
saxophone and a bull dog. Start with an account of
mediaeval sorcery and queer potations? Exactly, and
give away the story before it begins.

．　　　．　　　．　　　．　　　．　　　．　　　．

I had a dear old friend, a professor, who got a
brilliant idea (so he told me) for a mystery story, to
be laid in London. He began it by describing two
friends approaching London up the river on a steamer.
They never got there; they talked too much.

．　　　．　　　．　　　．　　　．　　　．　　　．

So suppose you turn and see how Robert Louis
Stevenson went at it . . . Wonderful, isn't it? From
the first word. And not a wasted sentence in the whole;
all done by the superb art of narration that only a
combination of initial talent and arduous exercise can
achieve.

．　　　．　　　．　　　．　　　．　　　．　　　．

Here is the outline of another plot-story which has
gone round the world as the *Prisoner of Zenda*.

The story opens with a careless but capable Englishman of good family, lazily cracking eggs at his lazy
breakfast. Now, though he doesn't know it, the careless gentleman has an extraordinary resemblance to a

careless, but worthless European reigning prince of
still better family. In fact they are absolute doubles.
This is not really so strange because, generations ago,
their families were one family. But they know nothing
of this. Mr. Rassendyll has never been in Ruritania
and Ruritania never heard of Mr. Rassendyll.

Then two things happen. The careless, over-care-
less, even dissolute prince is to be betrothed to a beautiful and related princess, an affair of state, not of
love. A rival court faction, dead set against the marriage, makes a plot to prevent the ceremony of betrothal by kidnapping the prince. That's one thing.
The other is that Mr. Rassendyll happens to take a
careless trip to Ruritania—knowing nothing of the
Prince or of the Princess Flavia or the approaching
betrothal—or anything. The prince gets kidnapped
and shut up in a castle (as the "Prisoner of Zenda").
But his adherents discover Mr. Rassendyll, the double
of the prince. He is substituted, or as they say in the
movies "stands in" for the Prince and is duly betrothed; the Princess indifferent to the real prince falls
in love with the substitute. After which one may easily
conceive the alarms and excursions, the terrific hit
made by Mr. Rassendyll as a reigning prince, the
advance thrill as the time draws near that will change
betrothal to marriage, rescue of the real prince, and
the renunciation and farewell of Rassendyll, ex-prince,
ending the story with Rassendyll back in England,
lazily cracking breakfast eggs again and reading newspaper items about the royal marriage in Ruritania.

.     .     .     .     .     .     .

But observe that if you, unless you are one in thousands, were given as a present the copyright of such a plot you could do nothing with it. You still have to *make* the characters. It's no use *saying* that Rassendyll is careless; you've got to make him careless. That's why Mr. Anthony Hope had him crack eggs in Chapter I. You wouldn't have thought of that. You would have given him orange juice and spoiled him. It's no use saying that the princess is charming; you got to prove it—which is harder than cracking eggs. After which you must make Black Michael black, and Reckless Rupert reckless and a lot of other things; get in colour without getting tiresome; make a big crowd in a few strokes and a grim castle in a couple of sentences.

.     .     .     .     .     .     .

Nor is that all that is to be said about plot and the positive difficulty of turning it into reality. There is on the other side the relative difficulty of keeping things out of it. A good story can be spoiled by the introduction of unnecessary elements, of secondary characters not needed and incidents only put in to fill up. In the egotism of creation a writer is apt to think too well of his characters; he gives us too much of them. They get tiresome.

A great many of the stories of yesterday (and even of today) were badly damaged by the tradition of the need for "comic relief." The idea of having comic people to take off the strain of the tragic people, the idea of contrast to heighten colour, came from the stage to the book. It is as old as Shakespeare. No doubt the Greeks had it. Perhaps it can be traced clear

back to the snake in the first book of Genesis. The
stage clung to it till yesterday. Many of us remember
the good old-fashioned play in which the heroine has
no sooner left the stage in a flood of heart-breaking
tears than in comes the comic butler, upsets a tray,
stubs his toe, and puts the house in a roar.

All through the nineteenth century this idea of variation and relief dominated story-telling. Even now, no
doubt, it affects the minds of many people who are
planning how to begin to write fiction. But it is wiser
to break away from it. Take your characters as they
come and take a chance on them. Some may be more
comic than you think.

.     .     .     .     .     .     .

Another myth of plot making is that if we take a
particular environment and tell all about it, it must be
interesting. It won't be, unless you can make it so.
Thus a writer lays his story on the east side of Chicago, or the west side of San Francisco, or among the
hay-makers of Indiana, or the cigar-makers of Omaha,
the head-hunters of Borneo or the pot-hunters of
Washington, the Manxmen of the Isle of Man, or the
brakesmen of the Nickel Plate Railway. This indeed
is what one may call the besetting sin of the fiction of
the present hour, or was proving itself so till war
bombed it to fragments. If it is gone, I for one am
glad. Life in odd places may be peculiar but I can do
without it. I've read enough. If there are any other
kind of farmers, share-croppers, hillbillies, mine workers and such, I'll do without them. I don't care how
hard they swear. I've heard enough. If that is an
exaggerated point of view let me restate it thus: A set

of people, any way of living, is not interesting in a literary sense unless it is made so by art. Without the art of narration each crowd is drearier than the last.

Another still heavier incubus that lies on fiction writing is the plan of following a man's life all through —every bit of it; how he had first lived on Chestnut Street in Philadelphia, and then moved to Walnut Street; first met Adelina Thompson and then threw her out and took in Adelina Jackson. A great many contemporary stories, some of the most successful, have been of this cradle-to-the-grave type. But in and of itself a cradle-to-the-grave story is not interesting. It still depends on how it is told. Living is one thing. Narrating life is another.

The test of the degree to which a writer possesses the art of narration can be made by imagining one page of his book missing and being asked to fill it in, having just the general idea of what it was about. With ninety per cent of our current stories there would be no great difficulty about this.

Thus let us say that the page before the missing one ended like this:

*"As Sir Everard entered the drawing room and advanced to meet his hostess, he saw before him"* . . .

No trouble here in going on. Give the woman's height, her breadth, thickness, estimate of her age, whether well-preserved or shot to pieces, complexion, teeth, and whether lame in one leg, and which. It is as simple as filling out a census form. But try to replace the description of Mr. Utterson, the lawyer whose portrait covers the opening page of *Dr. Jekyll and Mr. Hyde,*

and you would find that a very different matter; and
this, too, even if you had Mr. Utterson exactly in
your mind; you still must find the words, the way,
to put him over.

.    .    .    .    .    .    .

The reason why substitution is so easy in one case
and so hard in the other is that a poorly told story, or
even a story told moderately well, has so little depth
to it, that large stretches of it have no more character
to them than motor signs on a highway. They just
show where the story is going next.

.    .    .    .    .    .    .

One may well ask then: What must I do to be
saved? How can one acquire or cultivate this art of
narration? The answer is that the first thing to do is
to see how other people have succeeded. Open again,
with a new eye to see, some of the pages that have
seemed to you and to other people marvellously good
writing. Take a new look at Nathaniel Hawthorne
and Washington Irving and from then onwards to the
outstanding writers of the present hour; or select again
your favourites from the roll of honour of British
writers that runs from Walter Scott and Charles
Dickens down past Robert Louis Stevenson and Conan
Doyle and to the writers of today.

Here are some of the things you will note:

Good writers have a way of using the right word,
the word that exactly suits the sense, often so exactly
that its very exactness is pleasing to contemplate. Very
often, especially in the English language, there are half
a dozen words that will suit the sense in an approxi-
mate way, but none of which will convey exactly what

is meant. Lying aside in the corner of memory is the right word waiting to be rediscovered. One recalls J. M. Barrie's story of the little Scottish school boy who stuck dead in the middle of his composition while competing for a prize. He had been expected to win easily, but there he sat his head in his hands, tears gathering in his eyes—and not writing. Afterwards they asked him why; he said he wanted a word to describe how many people there were in church and he couldn't think of the right one. When they suggested this word or that he said no, that meant too many or too few. Then at last in a triumph that came too late he exclaimed, "A hantle! A 'hantle' of folk, that's what I meant."

It's a beautiful story, and one for a writer to ponder on. Barrie gives it as fiction; if it is not true, it ought to be.

But even harder than the choice of the right word, which is after all lying there ready to hand, is the construction of a combination of words that shall be striking, expressive, vivid; to make some happy phrase that fits an unusual adjective to a noun and thus gets one-and-one to make more than two. Consider the combination just used—"a happy phrase"—how happy it is, or once was, itself. To refer to a phrase thus, to personify it as if it sang with joy, is an act of constructive imagination. In such "happy" uses of words lay the genius of such a man as Chaucer, fashioning half-known words to the sudden expression of thought.

But the difficulty with striking phrases is that so many have struck so often that they are as it were "struck out." No spark comes; just a click. These combinations, once happy and expressive, have grown feeble with long service. These dead phrases are referred to in French as *clichés,* a word sometimes taken over into English. Those who wish to avoid the affectation of a foreign vocabulary sometimes call them *"chestnuts,"* a word of sudden and great vogue about fifty years ago but now itself a chestnut. Many writers on the use of English gather together for us lists of such worn-out phrases. A movement has been started in the columns of *John O' London,* that most admirable literary magazine, for the ejection of all such phrases out of use. Writers are invited to take an oath never to repeat them.

Many of the technical manuals on composition contain lists of these over-worked combinations. An excellent one is given by Mr. George B. Woods in his *Writers' Handbook* of 1922. Taking the *cliché* phrases out of these and similar lists we find that we could easily, if we wished, re-write our familiar literature with little other material.

Here for example is how *The Boy Stood on the Burning Deck:*

*The heroic youth stood on the deck already consigned to the flames. The devouring element gained apace. There was no friend in need; indeed help was conspicuous by its absence. There came a dull rumble, a terrific crash, followed by a sickening thud after which the boy's whereabouts became a matter of speculation.*

    •     •     •     •     •     •     •

Passing from the use of single words and verbal combinations, we find a field more difficult still in the use of comparison, as a means of forcible description of explaining a new thing from an old one, of making vivid the impression to be conveyed. Everyone who hasn't forgotten it remembers the difference between a simile, or open comparison in direct terms, saying that one thing is like another, and an indirect comparison by a metaphor which says that one *is* another. Thus the sentence *He rushed like a lion on the foe,* is a simile. The sentence *He rushed, a very lion, on the foe,* is a metaphor. Observe that literally a simile is the truth, and a metaphor is a lie. He wasn't really a lion; he was just so mad that he seemed like one. But the lie somehow wins out.

But whether lie or not, the use of metaphor is the very root of the growth of language. Biologists tell us how a piece of protoplasm in primitive life divides itself and then, as with the little nigger boy, walking in the zoo, then there are two. Perhaps it was the other way with the little niggers—there may have been *three* in the zoo—but anyway protoplasm makes two things out of one, then later specializes each portion to distinctive uses. Thus grows and multiplies organic nature. So it has been with language. Ever so many words, perhaps most of them, are just buried metaphor. Mountains are called "sierras" because they look like *saws.* A saw has *teeth.* A hammer has a *head,* and a ladder, though it has no head, has a *foot*—and so on endlessly. Such comparisons while still in the making are called slang. Once accepted, they are diction and get into the dictionary. Thus a hat is not yet officially a *lid,* nor a woman a *skirt* nor a man a *guy.* But fifty years hence they may become so. We may read for instance that the President of the United States, in receiving the British Ambassador, saw that the guy had a skirt with him and courteously lifted his lid. . . . A hundred years later still a skirt will be an old-fashioned courteous term for a lady of distinction, and a guy will mean a man like the president of Harvard or a judge of the Supreme Court.

. . . . . . .

A writer of today, John Brophy, in an interesting presentation of *English Prose* (1932) tells us that "the English language is strewn with the mummified corpses of once lively metaphors." Some he tells us have been so long dead that we have ceased to realize that they once were figurative. He quotes as an example the combination, *loud dress,* an epithet of sound applied to an object of sight, once full of life but now dead. Yet even this epithet might be resurrected. I remember once saying to a tailor (A.D. 1890) that I thought a certain material too loud. He replied that it was not so as he had made out of this same material a pair of pants for himself and was surprised *how quiet they were on the street.* Here is new life galvanized into the mummy.

. . . . . . .

But the point under discussion is that people learning to write must make their metaphors vivid but not exaggerated, striking but not preposterous. Above all they must learn to recognize and avoid the muddle of the mixed metaphor, a comparison which jumbles up the different senses, confounds sight with sound and both of them with touch. Extreme and even silly examples make clear the fallacy of the mixed metaphor.

A mixed metaphor arises in the following way. A comparison is good. A sustained comparison is better still. As an illustration:

*But let us clear the shale and débris of argument with which the surface of the subject is encumbered and come down to the bed rock of fact, upon which truth must rest.*

This is excellent. You can almost see someone shovelling it all up. But in using metaphors you must stick to the same one; if you call a thing bed rock don't shift it to a grain of mustard seed. If you say that science sheds its rays of light, don't say that presently the fowls of the air will rest on it. They won't. If you decide to be a wave, remain one; don't say that a wave of sympathy from America will dry the tears of Europe. It can't.

The pulpit seems for some reason or other to lend itself especially to the creation of mixed metaphors. It may be that the minds of the clergy are filled with the vivid imagery of the scriptures—the green pastures, the fountains, the shadows of great rocks in weary lands, the seeds that grow to great trees—so filled with them that extempore oratory has not time to sort them out. Hence, we hear them express the hope that the work begun today may kindle a spark which will only need watering to make it a great fire that will spread and multiply till all the fowls of the air can sit on it.

. . . . . . .

But even without actually mixing metaphor to the point of literary criminality many writers dull the point of their style with combinations that slur and confuse sense and sound and touch and shift incontinently from one to another.

*The chairman said that they must make a great effort, put their shoulders to the wheel and strike out with both hands, with their heads high.*

And so on. (Chairmen *often* talk this way.)

Yet everybody who writes will find that comparison is a powerful instrument and everybody who reads may judge how vital is its use.

You have only to open a page of Charles Dickens to realize the extraordinary use made by him of metaphor and simile. All description became comparison.

*"He was forever comparing everything with everything else,"* writes one of his many biographers, *"and, above all, in this way endowing inanimate objects with life and movement. For him, windows grin, doors yawn, clocks wink solemnly and trees talk in the night breeze. The fancies of Barnaby Rudge watching the clothes dance upon the clothes-line are those of his creator."*

At times such comparisons touch a note of such deep pathos that the sound lingers as part of Dickens's permanent legacy:

*What are the wild waves saying,*
*Sister, the whole day long?*

.    .    .    .    .    .    .

Often this sheer ingenuity of comparison becomes a vehicle of humour as when Dickens describes one of the cricket players of All-Muggleton as looking like half a roll of flannel, and another player as looking like the other half. Compare here Bill Nye's description of a man who had legs "like twenty-five minutes after six."

. . . . . . .

But there are other and more comprehensive aspects of the art, and especially of the method, of narration, still to be discussed. Consider, for example, the question of the narrator, that is, of who tells, or is supposed to tell, the story. The author can write his story in a purely impersonal way without stating how he came to know it. He writes it in this case with a sort of omniscience. He knows the secret feelings and thoughts of everybody; knows what's happening even when there are no witnesses, and of course knows what is going to happen and can't pretend that he doesn't. This is far and away the most usual method of story writing at the present time. Only a child would wonder how the writer came to know it all—only a child or the mythical young lady who wondered how the astronomers came to know the names of the stars. The vast advantage of this method lies in its omniscience. Such disadvantage as it has comes from the fact that it is after all only a chronicle—the record of something all done and finished and not of something happening now.

A second method, which today is the only serious competitor of the third person omniscient, is the plan of telling the story through the mouth of a character; of making it what is sometimes called a story with an *I* in it. This evidently makes for vividness and reality;

it sounds as if someone was telling the story to you. But unfortunately, *I* can't know everything; can only relate what *I* see and hear and what people tell *me,* and not what people say to one and another when *I*'m not there. But there is not only the value of directness, of living communication as it were, but also the fact that the character telling the story may be a creation through whose eyes we see things hidden from our own. Take the case of *Huckleberry Finn.* Here is a book which all admire and which many think the greatest work of fiction ever written in America. But the very essence of the book—and its chief merit—is that we look out on the world through Huck Finn's eyes. Our vision is refracted to that of the little outcast on his raft and all the world is changed. The simple elementary values of life, the natural estimates of good and bad, commonly lost in the shifting perplexed pattern of social existence, show clear again, as an X-ray. Huck can convey to us more about slavery and the old slave days in one sentence than a voluminous down-south novel in a whole chapter.

*"Anybody hurt?"*
*"No, Mum—killed a nigger."*

Sometimes, however, the *I* in the story is inserted merely as a background relator, a negative character, nobody particular in himself, who narrates the things that have happened to the people around him, of which he chanced to be a spectator. An elderly clergyman does nicely in this role; if not a clergyman then someone as neutral and insignificant as a presidential elector. Otherwise *I* may give offense by blowing *my* horn too much and, especially in an adventure story, by "hogging the whole show." One recalls the well-worn quotation: *Pierre was the bravest man in France; he said so, and he ought to know.* So it was that the *I* of the old-fashioned adventure story grew very tiresome; his excessive bravery was equalled only by his modesty; his way of almost giving himself up for lost (as when they tied him to the stake and lit the fire), all this was wonderful in the first exuberance of popular story-telling in the nineteenth century but has long since worn thin.

.         .         .         .         .         .         .

An obvious variation of the method of first person narration (the story with an *I* in it) is the method of a diary, or of a story written up in instalments. A diary, except in a limited capacity, is singularly hard to sustain; it has in it that peculiar artificiality already mentioned in an earlier chapter. People don't really chronicle things in diaries. Even the usual pretense that the writer writes his diary as a sort of solace to his loneliness or to divert his mind from his misfortunes doesn't quite wash. It was a favorite device, however, of earlier authors. But as a matter of fact this hug-the-diary to the heart is only suited for a prisoner in the Bastille writing: *Another day. A second rat appeared but refused all my efforts to coax him towards me. My other fly died last night.*

That's first rate and most suitable. So too is the diary the proper form for anything really and truly happening day by day, the kind of scope that an actual diary might fill. When *Gentlemen Prefer Blondes* they naturally prefer them from day to day. Another method, a novelty till it was overworked, is to cast a story in the form of letters. The advantage is that we can thus have two—or more—points of view instead of that of one narrator. The disadvantage is that the movement is apt to be slow—and the form itself, when it runs down to *From the same to the same* . . . gets tiresome. Yet Ring Lardner showed how genius can use it to reveal people's characters by the way they write letters. (See his story—*Some Like Them Cold*.)

.    .    .    .    .    .    .

In the old-fashioned novel writing the writer was seldom content to stand entirely outside of his picture. Quite apart from any narration by a character in the first person, he had a way of stepping in and out of the story himself, and inviting his reader to observe *this* and to notice *that,* and adjuring him not to think so and so or to conclude something else; or, if the story seemed to be getting dull, to cheer the reader up with the assurance of lots more things coming. The author of the period especially loved to address the person whom he called "my fair reader." This was a sort of come-along compliment to the dumpy, sentimental ladies of forty-five who were more apt to be reading a three-decker novel than would a fly-away girl of fifteen. The "fair reader" in that case was at least flattering; but not so applicable to a grimy old miner reading a paper novel in a log cabin. But to the Victorians it was all one. These superficial tricks of writing, in reality matters that lie upon the surface and are no deeper than passing fashion, now-a-days put us off the older books. Unless appreciated when young an effort is required to "get into them."

Much deeper than fashion and below the surface in the very life of fiction is the varying method of relation that corresponds to what we may call *tone*—for want of a better word. If *tune* may be used, as we have used it above, for the run of the words and sentences, then *tone* may serve to indicate the difference of the author's voice in the relation; whether he throws into it the sentiment of what he relates or relates it only as it happens—the difference between romance and realism, between sentiment and statement, fantasy or photograph. French writers and French critics have analyzed and discussed this aspect of fiction far more than we have in English, and have been far more self-conscious in regard to it. Students of writing should get a clear idea of what is meant here by *romantic,* a thing very different from the wider and more usual meaning of romantic. The two are cognate but not the same. When we talk of romantic scenery we mean scenery which suggests and suits strange stories, scenery where lovers might have walked and wooed—a glade in a green wood, a forsaken garden, a broken mill, a ruined castle —as distinct from a city street beside a stock exchange. Wherever love may sigh (in suitable sighing places), or danger lurk, or gallantry defy it—wherever golden fortune breaks the closed circuit of daily life—there is romance. To its portrayal the world has devoted the softest of its music, the most appealing of its poetry, most stirring of its dramas and the thousand and one tales of its imagination.

When we speak of romantic writing, we recall the heroes and the heroines of Walter Scott or the figures (wax and otherwise) of Tennyson's *Idylls of the King*. To what extent such people as Tennyson's "Blameless King Arthur" are possible, what difference there is (if any) between King Arthur and a stuffed shirt, is another matter. To the proper kind of reader of their day, if they were not true to life they were at least much better than life. Ordinary life, as compared with them, was as a ham sandwich to a banquet.

But it is also possible to write stories about people who live not in castles, but on Main Street and fall in love with people as commonplace as themselves. Stories in fact can be told all the way from cowboys and cabbages up to kings. Everybody understands in a general way the difference between romantic and realistic stories, tales of life as it might be and narratives of life as it is.

But a further difference comes up when we refer not to the subject and characters of a story, but the way of writing it. It would be possible, in this sense, to write romantically of very poor and simple people, as Dickens often did, or to write realistically of kings and castles as many writers try to do now. In this sense romantic writing means a way of telling a story in which the author's own feeling and sentiments blend with and colour the narrative. The realistic way of telling a story is to state the facts and not to weep or laugh over them, not to express approval or disapproval, but to leave that to the reader. Take a simple example:

*The poor old man thus found himself out in the bitter cold with no home to go to etc. etc.*

Observe the word *poor;* that's the author's opinion about the old man, expressing his sympathy for him. A realist wouldn't call him that, unless he meant the word in the other sense as *penniless,* to express a fact. But observe also the word *bitter;* that is all right here even for a realist because it refers presumably to the thermometer. But if we wrote *the cruel cold,* that would be romantic writing. In other words the ideal of the realist writer is to make a purely impersonal picture (a photograph) a purely impersonal narrative (a record).

The difference between the two methods and the conscious cultivation of either has been much more emphasized in France than in England. Indeed this field of art became for a time a sort of battleground of rival schools. The writer whose name is chiefly connected with realistic style is Guy de Maupassant who practised it with a perfection of technique seldom attained. Students of the art of writing may turn to the story *La Parure* (*The Necklace*) as a perfect specimen of his work.

In Britain and in America the fiction of the nineteenth century was overwhelmingly romantic in method, though rather by instinct than by art. But in the twentieth century the tendency has been more the other way, though the two methods of treatment have always blended and intermingled. Dickens, for example, was overwhelmingly romantic; the very life of his stories is the colour of sentiment, of approval or disapproval that runs through them. He joins his readers in roars of laughter or sobs of tears at his characters. He would put in such epithets as the "noble

Mrs. Gamp," the "magnanimous Mr. Pecksniff"—
which have nothing to do with the story but just comment on the character, and that a satirical one. Yet Dickens at times wrote pages of realism—clear, direct and wonderful in its appeal. Turn to the account of Mr. Dorrit's sudden mental seizure at his own grand banquet, when his mind carries him again to the Marshalsea prison and his horrified guests see him rise and call to his daughter in perplexity, "Amy, is Joe on the lock?" There is no "poor Dorrit" in this, no Dickens so to speak, no comment and none needed, just a picture, a record, tragic and overwhelming in the plain truth of its narration.

Now as a matter of fact it is not possible to separate realistic writing completely from romantic. The very facts that the writer selects imply a preference over other facts. The writer thinks them more interesting. If Guy de Maupassant hadn't thought the idea of *La Parure* pathetic he wouldn't have written it. After all heroism will out, tears will flow and have done so ever since the Roman poet said "the world is full of weeping" (*sunt lachrymae rerum*)—and even before. The stock in trade of the romanticists is part of human nature itself. We come to it by instinct. Our "boys' stories," as Mr. Chesterton once said in a wonderful phrase, "still drive their dark trade in heroes."

But the valid basis of realism is its protest against the exaggerated sentiment, the "sob-stuff," the mock heroism and the stock heroism into which treatment can so easily degenerate. The Victorian age loved tears, even when it did not propose to wipe them away. Barefooted street boys, emaciated chimney-sweeps, girls stitching a shirt as a prelude to throwing themselves into the Thames, fathers who refuse to come home from a saloon even when sung to—all this drew ready tears. Tears are indeed of the very fountain of life. But there is danger in them. We may be led to substitute weeping for action, and sympathy for relief. One is apt to suspect that the Victorians felt as if their flood of generous tears had washed them free from obligations.

In our more realistic age we are impatient of impotent weeping. We are apt to say, "Stop crying about it and see what can be done." Hence we change the *Song of the Shirt* to the plain talk of a minimum wage statute, and try at least, to drag father out of the saloon with a prohibition law. "Tears, idle tears, and yet I know not why," said the Victorian. He seemed to sit and gulp, and like himself for it. We want to know why, and if we fail today we mean to succeed tomorrow, even if it is a long tomorrow in coming. Yet it is hard to judge. There are dangers both ways. It may be that tears water the flowers of life and feed the roots of action. Some of the Victorian sobs and songs —like the *Song of the Shirt* itself—helped to make the world's history. The new use now beginning to be made of this very term realistic shows where the new danger may lie. A *realistic* point of view, to our newspapers at any rate, now means one that depends on fact and force, and not upon agreement or obligation by honour. A realist is becoming the new name for the man who used to be called an "unprincipled scoundrel."

As with the sobs of grief so with the ecstasies of love. The romanticist and the realist try to capture them, each in his own way. The Victorian age loved love as it loved tears. Hence, its impossible heroines who became a stock-in-trade of nineteenth century fiction. The heroine had to combine an ideal beauty, an impeccable virtue, a modesty and an innocence that ran idiocy hard.

There was no attempt to make the heroines true to life. They were supposed to be better than life. As the reader liked them that way then no harm was done and everybody was pleased. To all her other graces the heroine added a power of language rarely found outside of a legislative assembly. This was her weapon with which she could compel even the blackest villain to "unhand her." Here, as an example, is one of Charles Dickens' earlier heroines (Kate Nickleby) telling her wicked uncle "where he gets off at":

" 'In the meantime,' interrupted Kate, with becoming pride and indignation, 'I am to be the scorn of my own sex, and the toy of the other; justly condemned by all women of right feeling, and despised by all honest and honourable men; sunken in my own esteem, and degraded in every eye that looks upon me. No, not if I work my fingers to the bone, not if I am driven to the roughest and hardest labour. Do not mistake me, I will not disgrace your recommendation. I will remain in the house in which it placed me, until I am entitled to leave it by the terms of my engagement; though, mind, I see these men no more! When I quit it, I will hide myself from them and you, and, striving to support my mother by hard service, I will live, at least, in peace, and trust in God to help me.' "

But if the romantic heroine is unsatisfactory, what about the realist one? If we are to portray the heroine just as she is, what is left of her? You cannot depict love inside a frame of fact. It needs a mist to dissolve in. You cannot tell a love story just as it is—because it isn't. There is something else there, something higher than our common selves and perhaps truer. When a young man sees in his girl an angel, and a young girl sees in her lover a hero, perhaps they are seeing what is really there—the self we each might have but which we grasp only in our higher moments and too late. Hence you cannot in the art of narration bind love within the fetters of fact. It slips through as easily as radio through a prison wall. A "realistic" love story is either grubby, or false, or both. It is probable that the distorted image of a Kate Nickleby is nearer to what a young man sees when in love, than any picture that can be drawn by loveless observation.

With that one comes back round the circle of discussion that revolves round realism and romance.

．　　．　　．　　．　　．　　．　　．

People who want to write fiction should ponder deeply on these aspects of imaginative writing. It is all very well to speak of unconscious art, as if a writer with the proper gift would find a way to write, as a bird finds a way to sing. In a sense he will. But after all a great many birds sing badly. Any crow would have been much the better for a few lessons. The mocking laugh of the loon of the Canadian lakes, with just a little more training, would be valuable on the platform—and invaluable among the audience. Indeed most birds stop just where they ought to begin. So t is with writers. Only the greater are above the need for conscious and conscientious effort . . . and generally they use it most.

.    .    .    .    .    .    .

The description of scenes and of persons, of wind and weather becomes an essential part of the art of narration. It gives the background of the stage where fiction walks. The cultivation of the art of description becomes a very necessary part of training in writing. The first thing, however, to remember is that description—outside of a summer resort folder or a public list of persons wanted—is not the main purpose of fiction. It is an adjunct, not an end itself. It ought, therefore, never to be allowed to overdo its part. One of the worst and one of the most irritating errors in the use of description is to allow the description to block the current of the narrative and bring it to a full stop, just as the reader's interest and excitement is being carried forward with a rush.

This is seen especially in the detective story in connection with "the finding of the body." There is a standardized scene in which Inspector Higginbottom and various attendant characters decide to break in the door of the library, convinced that Sir Charles must be lying murdered in the room within. They break it in (Higginbottom does it with his shoulder; always at the third heave); what do they find? The body? No—this:

*The room thus revealed appeared of a size considerably larger than a less considerable room, rectangular in shape, its walls lined with books except on the north side which gave on to the garden!*

(The body! The body! Never mind what gave on what— Was the body there?)

. . . . . . *A large old-fashioned fireplace, the mantelpiece of which might easily have been Georgian, if not Jacobean, gave up the chimney* . . .

But the body! Wasn't it there?

Oh, yes, Sir Charles is there all right, lying across the hearth rug, dead. His body is the first thing which anybody, except a detective story author, would see. But the author will only find it after crawling all round the room first.

Such a method is admirable for filling up space so as to turn a ten-thousand-word story into a seventy-thousand-word book. The natural length of a crime story—based on the time during which you can hold your breath, the period of sustained attention—is about ten thousand words. That, however, is a bad length— commercially—too long for an article, too short for a book. Hence the enormous quantity of needless descriptive material written into crime stories to fatten them out. One favorite British author of the day takes care to lay his stories in market-towns dating from the Crusades. In an English market-town it takes twenty pages of description to work one's way up the High Street. Even then there's still the Keep, and the Close and the Crypt.

As compared with the swift unerring power of description in true art such a mass of needless undigested detail is deplorable. It is not possible to call up vividly a scene in nature, a lonely wood, a windswept shore, a wild dark night—but by putting it together item by item. One grain of sand and then another grain of sand won't make a desert. You cannot describe a house brick by brick, nor a wood leaf by leaf. Yet that is the method adopted, especially in poetry, by all of our second-rate writers, and accepted by some even of our first. Real descriptive power shows things in a flash— like a carriage wheel seen by lightning, or at least in a single sustained focus, not in a mosaic of little sections. Take this for example (It is from the pen of Austin Dobson.) as a vivid picture of a dead soldier lying in a wood:

> *Here in this leafy place,*
> *Quiet he lies.*

Observe the art of it—*in this leafy place*—the rest of it left to the reader's own imagination. Your leafy place may be very different from my leafy place, but all are beautiful.

Take this:

> *In Flanders fields the poppies blow*
> *Between the crosses row on row.*

How many of us can recall our first reading of John McCrae's immortal verse—the whole scene pictured in those two marvellous lines.

Even single phrases happily chosen and blending metaphor with fact may carry a marvellous descriptive power, such as seen in the scriptural phrases of King James's Bible . . . *the shadow of a great rock in a weary land*—the word *weary* carries with it a wide vision, a desolation. *A rushing, mighty wind* . . .

But it must be remembered that good description can never be effected by mere oddity of detail, or mere accuracy of observation with nothing else in it except accuracy. At times a poetical genius uses a description which turns on some nice observation of sights and sounds which each of us has made perhaps, but only in an unconscious way. The shock of recognition renders vivid what is meant. Thus, Tennyson:

*Her feet have touched the meadows and have left the daisies rosy.*

That is, the pink side of the daisies shows when they are turned over in the morning dew. Of course, says the reader, so they are, and recalls a hundred mornings of his own lazy uninventiveness.

But no amount of such oddity of detail is of any value in description of itself, not unless it is a thing that the reader himself has seen and known . . . It is no use to talk with marvellous accuracy of the underside of an aspen leaf, or the top layer of a toad-stool unless there is significance and recognition. Our poets and perhaps especially over in Canada—if I may dare lump them together in sin—have erred especially in this respect. They have picked our words to pieces twig by twig, dissected them leaf by leaf and for the most part got no further.

I am well aware that exception might be taken to this apparent denunciation of lengthy descriptive passages. I might be reminded of the use of sustained description by those great writers of fiction in the nineteenth century both in Britain and America whom we begin now to regard in retrospect as classics. Here are Fenimore Cooper's matchless descriptions of the primeval forest in which lurk the last, and the worst of his Mohicans; or his wonderful sea pictures of the days of the full-rigged ships staggering under a cloud of sail. We think of Washington Irving, and feel drowsy at the very thought of Sleepy Hollow. Even more intimately do we connect Sir Walter Scott with the Highland pictures of "Caledonia stern and wild."

But mere accumulation of detail can never carry this descriptive power. It becomes merely one example, one subdivision of the general dulness that goes with garrulousness of all kinds—too many words for too little said. But the point is one to reserve for the later discussion of how not to write poetry.

.    .    .    .    .    .    .

Everybody knows how garrulous old people become in their conversation. They can't begin without going backwards and beginning again; they can't end because there is always something more to say. Their talk is their first taste of eternity. Time is fading; it no longer matters.

Now there is the same garrulousness in writing. Pecuniary motives favor it since a "book" needs two dollars and fifty cents' worth of words to make it, commercially, a book. One can understand, too, that authors paid by the word naturally tend to get prosy. There used to be in bygone days a set of writers, hired to write stories and paid by the line, "penny-a-liners," they were called. Naturally their stories ran to such dialogue as the following:

*The rivals met:—*
*Hold, sirrah!*
*Who bids me hold?*
*I!*
*You?*
*Yes!*
*Ha!*
*Bah!*
*Yah!*
*Draw!*
The steel clashed.

We can laugh at the mote in the eye of the penny-a-liner but the beam is at times in our own. Even quite apart from any peculiar motive, sheer conceit favors a garrulous style. The writer seems to hug himself over each sentence, expanding it and keeping his story waiting while he lingers over it.

Here is how it is done:

Let us say that the statement to be made is, *Father decided not to shave till after dinner.*

Here's how it is expanded into garrulousness:

*An important question now arose. The problem was whether father should shave before dinner or wait till dinner was finished and then shave after it was over. Either course presented certain definite advantages. But on the other hand each alternative was accompanied by certain equally definite disadvantages. To shave before dinner had the advantage of getting it over and done with. Yet it involved an initial effort, a firm determination and a resolute execution. In other words it was a nuisance. Nor could it be done by halves. As against this, even if father did not shave before dinner, he would still have to shave after dinner—or else go to bed in his whiskers. The difficulty would merely grow with delay. In the end, after much cogitation and many half-formed resolves, father decided not to shave till after dinner.*

But is the garrulous writer done with it at this? Oh, no, he goes right on:

*Had father known what profound consequences were involved in this seemingly simple postponement, he would have . . .*

Quite so. He'd have cut his throat in despair. But we don't care if he does.

These fits of long-windedness are due, I repeat, very likely far more to the conceit of authorship than to motives of advantage. The writer thinks the situation so interesting that he loves to dwell on it. These interpolations, so fascinating to the author, are the parts of stories that people skip. Indeed the skipping habit arose out of their existence. An analysis of them would show that they occur and recur in regulation situations, as when the heroine wonders whether what she is making of her life is what her life ought to be made; or when the great detective having viewed the body starts to play the concertina.

. . . . . . .

There is a queer elusive quality that makes for success in the art of narration which one may call, for lack of a better name, verisimilitude. No rule can be given for how to achieve it. But, as with all other factors, the recognition that it is there to achieve, is the first step towards its achievement. It means the power of making a thing *seem* true, even though it isn't. It carries a sort of sincerity about it by putting into the narrative a certain amount of exactness of dates and details. In and of themselves a mere mass of dates and details will never help to make fiction sound like truth. A story that begins with an elaborate family tree is unconvincing from the start. It doesn't make the existence of Mr. Hewetson (in Chapter One) any more real to us to say that his name was really Huitson, and that his great-grandfather had been in the Baltic timber trade, but had changed his name when he went into the Newfoundland fish business. Nor does it help to say that he may have got some part of his character from his maternal grandmother. He may. I don't care if he did. That sort of overdone accuracy and superfluous detail falls flat.

I always think that Conan Doyle possessed this quality, this ability to seem to tell the truth in a high degree. He showed it especially with his Sherlock Holmes stories. He did it with incidental touches, put in after this fashion:

*It was, if I remember rightly, on the evening of the day when Holmes had just been awarded the Rumford medal . . . etc. . . .*

Observe the phrase, *if I remember rightly*. That is to say, it may have been a different evening, or a dif-

ferent medal but at any rate it was one of those eve-
nings and one of those medals. This sounds truer than
truth. Indeed Conan Doyle stuffed so much verisimilitude into Sherlock that he presently stepped out of
Conan Doyle's pages and took on an existence of his
own. The story is often told of how little French boys,
visiting London and being driven about the town,
wanted eagerly to see the place where Sherlock Holmes
lived. For the Latin Americans in South America Sherlock Holmes has become an entity in himself, a legend-
ary character like King Arthur, about whom anybody
may write stories. Conan Doyle was merely the first
person who wrote about him. Under such universal
treatment Sherlock Holmes no doubt would ultimately
go to pieces like that tiresome half-dog, half-public
nuisance that began so wonderfully as Tarzan. This
attitude towards Sherlock bears evidence to the
extraordinary amount of concentrated creation that
was put into him. This may have been one of the reasons why, if the current story is true, Conan Doyle
got sick of Sherlock, grew, one might say, to hate him
—in fact was jealous of him. Doyle killed him once
by throwing him over a cliff in Switzerland, but back
he came; Doyle later on shot him, crippled him, turned
his hair white—but it was no good. Sherlock beat him
in the end.

I know of no fictitious character of the present hour
who has thus, as it were, acquired an independent life,
unless it be Charlie McCarthy. Whatever Mr. Bergen
may claim in the matter, it has become clear that
Charlie is a personality by himself with an independent

mind and character. If precedent holds good his creator will become jealous of him, as Conan Doyle did
of Sherlock, and may try to make an end of him.
Charlie should be warned in time.

.    .    .    .    .    .    .

How strange it is, to think of these characters of
fiction—from the Charlie McCarthys and the Mr.
Chipses and Mrs. Minivers of the present hour—back
to the Huck Finns and the Pickwicks, all the way to
Shakespeare . . . Their lives in a way more real than
what is round us—at least more known, and warmer
. . . The person who can still, as the years pass on,
be "buried in a book" (note the method; buried; lost
to the world) is fortunate indeed.

.    .    .    .    .    .    .

It is all very well, however, to say make your fiction
sound like truth. The trouble is to do it. Only Ulysses
could bend Ulysses's bow. But a writer may at least,
if he cannot make falsehood sound like truth, avoid
making truth sound like falsehood. Very many true
anecdotes, memories and reminiscences are deprived
of all appearance of truth by the manner of narrating
them. The writer feels that he must suppress all references to actual places and actual people not necessary
for his story—and in doing this reduces the story to
a nullity. *"The most remarkable linguist I ever knew,*
he writes, *"was a bishop of a certain church whom I
will just call Bishop Q. I remember dining with him at
the house of my friend F. where there was also in the
company one of the most distinguished wits of the
London bar whom I will merely designate as Wit. X.*

*X. asked Q. his opinion of the great philologist P.H.,
and Q. . . ."*

Quite so, but never mind what he answered. Better
call the bar just B., and call the dinner off; there is no
interest in any story told that way.

# CHAPTER VI

## GOOD AND BAD LANGUAGE

*English superiority and American slang — The English steal the language, the Americans the continent — Canadians and Eskimos out of it — Luxuriance of American slang — Seventeen kinds of guys in one Wisconsin high school — American sky-pilots and British incumbents — The New Realism — A hero with guts — How to swear in print — Foul oaths, then fouler and foulest — The panorama man and the peasant in the Swiss More-Ass*

QUITE apart from the technical aspect of the art of narration, there is the broader general question of good and bad language, of where speech ends and slang begins. To what extent must the language of literature and cultivated discourse accept and assimilate the innovations, the irregularities and the corruptions that perpetually appear in all languages as spoken by the mass of the people? To what extent are we to think of our language as a moving current, never the same except in its identity, and to what extent should we wish to check the flow of the current, so that stiller waters may run deeper! Obviously there is a limit in each direction. A current totally arrested means stagnation. Waters that run too fast end in the sand. Somewhere there may be a happy mean between the two.

Now this question arises for all languages. But it has

a very peculiar importance for the English language since here the current flows in two parts, the American and the British; and many people are inclined to think that one tends to run too fast and the other tends to slacken. In other words we have here the problem of the American language and American slang. Every now and then controversy breaks out in regard to British English and American English—or it used to before the war stilled all babble—and it sometimes had a rather nasty edge to it. It carried in it one of the last faint survivals of the Stamp Act and the Boston Tea Party. Great quarrels die away to leave only generous memories; little quarrels live on. Hence the question of "slang" as between England and America (England, not Scotland; the Scots are not worrying) keeps its edge; all the more so, in that a lot of Americans think in their hearts, that the reason why the English don't use much slang is that they can't make it up, and a lot of English people think that the Americans use slang because they weren't brought up properly —or, no, they don't think it, they know it. That's the provoking thing about the English (say the Americans); they don't think things, they know them. They did all their thinking years and years ago.

I can write on this controversy with the friendly neutrality of a Canadian. In Canada we have enough to do keeping up with two spoken languages without trying to invent slang, so we just go right ahead and use English for literature, Scotch for sermons and American for conversation.

Perhaps the highest point of controversy is reached in the discussion whether there is, whether there ought to be, whether it is a shame that there isn't, an "American" language. Some people feel very strongly on this point. They think that having your own language is a mark of independence like owning your own house, driving your own car and having your own shaving mug in the barber shop. Gangs of boys make themselves up a "language" and revel in its obscurity. The leading boys in the respect are the Irish, so anxious to have their own language that they are trying to learn Gaelic. If they are not careful, first thing they know they'll get to talk it and then they'll be sorry.

On the other hand, some people feel just the other way about it. A most interesting article appeared a little while ago in one of the leading British Quarterlies, written by an American, and deprecating all idea of the creation of an American language as dangerous to our mutual dependence and kinship.

My own feeling about this, if I may put it in slang, is "I should worry." Or, in other words, there is not the faintest chance of there ever being an American language as apart from English. The daily intercommunication of telegraph, telephone, literature and the press, fuses all forms of "English" toward one and the broadcast and the talking pictures even fuse the toned voice. In the world of today languages cannot separate. That process belonged to epochs of distance and silence unknown now. Even then it was long. It took Latin a thousand years to turn into French.

The situation in the world today is this: There is a language called "English." It is too bad, if you like that one country should seem to have stolen or to monopolize the claim to the name. But if the English stole the name of a language, the "Americans" stole the whole of two continents. Humble people, like the Canadians, and the Eskimos, have to live in "America" and speak "English," without fretting about it.

English is spoken by the people in England; is also spoken by the Scots, by the unredeemed Irish, the Australians—a lot of other people than Americans. Who speaks it best, no one knows; it's a matter of taste. Personally I think I like best the speech of a cultivated Scot, and perhaps least a certain high-grade English which calls a railroad a "wailwoad." I myself talk Ontario English; I don't admire it, but it's all I can do; anything is better than affectation.

Now by slang is meant the unceasing introduction into language of new phrases, and especially new nouns as names for things. There is no doubt that this peculiar fermentation of language has reached in America higher proportions than ever known anywhere else. For example—and my authority here is Mr. Eric Partridge, who cannot be wrong—a test was taken not long ago in a Wisconsin high school to see how many different words the boys and girls employed to express a low opinion of a person. Their list reads, *mutt, bonehead, guy, carp, highbrow, tightwad, grafter, hayseed, hot-air artist, rube, tough-nut, chump* and *peanut*. Perhaps they thought of more after they got home; these no doubt were only some of the things they called their teachers.

Many people, without being students of language, have observed the extraordinary number of ways in which American slang can indicate that a man has had too much drink. The chief authority on the subject (I refer to American slang and don't want to be ambiguous), H. L. Mencken, gives a partial list, brought up to 1923, and including *piffled, fiddled, spiflicated, tanked, snooted, stewed, ossified, slopped, jiggered, edged, loaded, het up, frazzled, jugged, soused, cornered* and *jagged.*

Slang passes as it comes. It lives only when it deserves to live, when the word has something about it that does a real service. In the Wisconsin students' list above I can detect only two words that look permanent, *guy* and *highbrow. Guy* is a word with a history; it comes down to us from poor Guy Fawkes (Guido Faukes), tortured and executed for trying to blow up the English Parliament. His "Fifth of November" crime was kept alive in memory—still is—by toting around a tattered figure on a stick in a procession with the cry, "Oh, please to remember the fifth of November, with gunpowder, treason and plot." So the word came to mean a tattered-looking person and then just a queer-looking person, like a professor. From that it began to mean just a person: *I was out with another guy last night.*

The fact is we are always hard up for neutral words to mean "just a person"; each new one gets spoiled and has to be replaced. Be careful how you call a "woman" a "woman," and a "lady" is apt to be worse; don't call a Frenchman an "individual," or an Englishman a "fellow." Hence the need for "guy," which will gradually rise from ridicule to respectability, as already indicated in the chapter above. At some future British coronation the Archbishop of Canterbury will say to the Queen, "Will you take this guy to be your

husband?" And for all we know the Queen will answer, "Sez-you."

The other word, *highbrow*, will live for another reason. We need it. It is a little different from *intellectual,
learned, cultivated*. It started like most slang as a brilliant image, or metaphor, taken from the sweeping
forehead, smooth as an egg, of a Shakespeare or a
Hall Caine. But, with perhaps a change of spelling,
the thought of *brow* will disappear and we shall use
the term naturally and effectively—a *highbrow audience;* the *opinion of highbrows*, etc.

The making of slang is, as I say, a sort of living
process of language like the scum on wine. Without
it there is no wine, no life, no fermentation. Later on,
the scum passes as dust and dregs and leaves behind
the rich fluid of the wine. A language that has ceased
to throw off slang has ceased to live. Thus came all
our language. Every syllable of it since the dawn of
speech has been rolled over and over in endless re-
newal. Our oldest words, our oldest names, were once
bright with the colours of the morning, striking some
new metaphor that brought into full relief the image
of the thing seen. Centuries ago some Roman called
his fellow-Roman's head a "pot" and put the word
*testa* (tête) into the French language. His genius for
seeing resemblances was no greater than that of his
American successor who perceived that the human
head was a *bean*.

Now, the process of creating slang is not confined
to America. But I think the fermenting, slang-making
process is livelier far in America than in England. This
would seem to be the consequence of setting a language

in a new country—with new lives, new scenes to turn it to, and with the débris of other languages jostling beside it. Under the wide canopy of heaven above the prairies a preacher became a *sky-pilot*. In England he remained, among other things, an *incumbent*, still sitting there. A newcomer in the West was a *tenderfoot* or a *greenhorn*, a locomotive an *iron horse*, and so on. Little snips of foreign *idiom* like the *something else again* of German, and the *I should worry* of Yiddish, came snuggling into the language. *Yes, we have no bananas* carries with it the whole Mediterranean migration.

This process of change, like invention itself, became much more conscious in America than in England. What the English did for lazy convenience or by accident, the Americans did on purpose. Hence American slang contains a much greater percentage of cleverness than English. A lot of English slang words are just abbreviations. To call a professional at cricket a *pro*, or breakfast *brekker*, or political economy *pol. econ.*, saves time but that is all. To call a pair of trousers *bags*, is a step up; there is a distinct intellectual glow of comparison. But it is only twilight as compared with such American effects as *lounge-lizard*, *rubber-neck*, *sugar-daddy*, *tangle-foot* and *piece of calico*.

It is, moreover, a peculiar merit of American slang that a lot of it has the quality of vitality—vital force of renewed life. Take such words as a *hide-out* and *frame-up*, or a *tie-up* (on a railway). To make these involves the process of *starting over again*, forming language from the beginning. Compare *sob-stuff*, *fade-out*, *send-off*, *side-track* and a host of others.

Everything, as the French say, has the defects of its merits. American slang forces the pace, and hence a lot of it *is* forced, pointless, of no literary or linguistic value. Especially tiresome is the supposed slang of the criminal class, as used in crime novels to heighten the reader's terror. Every one recognizes such language as *See here, pal, if the narks grab you for doing in that moll, the beak will send you up, see, and you'll burn.* I don't know whether any people really use this stuff. I hope not. If they must be criminals, they might at least talk like gentlemen. But in any case English crime stories often run to the same kind of stuff; indeed I am not sure just where the words above belong.

But no one need be afraid that slang will really hurt our language, here or in England. It cannot. There is no dictatorship behind it. Words and phrases live only on their worth; they survive only on their merits. Nor does slang tend to separate America and England. As a matter of fact, the rising generation in England reach out eagerly for American slang. If that means they're not rising but sinking, it's too bad. But anyway we'll sink together.

.　　.　　.　　.　　.　　.　　.

So much for the toleration of slang as bad language turning into good, or dying from its very badness. What are we to say of bad language in the other sense, the kind that really is bad? Are we to put it in or leave it out? When we write a story our characters, if they are what are called "red-blooded" men and women, are apt to get profane; and even if they are thin-blooded they are apt to get nasty, in fact the thinner the nastier. The problem which all writers of fiction have to try to solve, and none have solved yet, is how to swear in print. Some writers of today think that they can solve the problem by ignoring it—just go ahead and swear. We open the pages of a typical novel and our eyes bounce off with a start at the expression . . . *You miserable bastard!* . . .

This is not said to the reader. It is what the hero says to, or rather *throws at* the villain, who has said something unbecoming in the presence of a girl, something that a girl ought not to hear. The hero is a splendid fellow. He has *guts*. The book says so. In fact that's why the girl likes him. It says, "She threw her arms about his neck and pressed her slim body close to him. 'You have guts,' she murmured." You see, she herself is so awfully slim that naturally—well, you get the idea. If not, you can read it all for yourself in any new book, under such a title as *Angel Whispers,* or *Undertones* or something like that, on the outside. On the inside it's full of *guts*. The new books are like that.

But we are not talking about any particular book but about the problem that is suggested—the question of how to deal with profanity in fiction—how can you swear in print?

.  .  .  .  .  .  .

We must, I fear, dismiss at once the old-fashioned Victorian expedient of telling the reader that one of the characters in the story said something "with a terrible oath." That won't do now-a-days. We want to hear it. What was it? This formula was the one used in the pirate stories written for boys and girls.

For example:

"Har! har!" shouted the pirate with a foul oath.

"They are in our power."

"They certainly are," said the second pirate with an oath fouler than the first.

"I'll say so," said the third pirate with an oath fouler still—a lot fouler.

The fourth pirate remained silent. He couldn't make it.

.    .    .    .    .    .    .

Now that won't do. We'll judge for ourselves how foul the oath is. If you can't say it, just whisper it. It's got to be pretty foul to get past us.

And I need hardly say, that it won't do to fall back on that old-fashioned trick that is used in novels "laid" in the Middle Ages—I mean the trick of making up a lot of fanciful stuff and calling it swearing.

Here's how it runs:

"Odd's piddlekins," cried Sir Gonderear, "by my halidome, thou art but a foul catiff. Let me not, or I'll have at you."

"Nay, by the Belly of St. Mark," answered the Seneschal, "I fear thee not, false paynim . . . Have one on me!" (Or words to that effect.) That was all right, as we shall see in the discussion of historical romances, from Sir Walter Scott. It won't do now. Such an epithet as *foul catiff* has been replaced by *you big stiff*, and a *paynim* is a *lobster*.

.    .    .    .    .    .    .

There used to be a special kind of swearing reserved by convention for the use of sailors in sea-stories. "Shiver my timbers!" cried the bosun, "you son of a swob! Lift a finger, you lobscouse, and I'll knock the dead lights out of you." After which he spat a quid—

a *quid pro-quo*—into the lee scuppers.

Fenimore Cooper is a case in point. The public of his day was too strict in its ideas to allow a sailor even to shiver his timbers in print. A glance at any of Cooper's famous sea stories will reveal such terrible profanity as d—l, apparently hinting at *devil,* and d—e, which may be interpreted with a thrill as "damme." Oddly enough, in Cooper's day the word "bloody" had not yet taken on in America its later offensive connotation, so that Cooper was at liberty to write, "D—e," said the bosun, "what the d—l does the bloody fellow mean?" But we may leave that to Fenimore Cooper. At present you couldn't navigate even a car ferry with a truck on it on that language.

You see, it was much easier to get away with such things a hundred years ago, at the beginning of modern fiction, than it is now. Take the case of Charles Dickens. He couldn't, of course, put real swearing into his books, and anyway he wouldn't have wanted to. So he set up a sort of jargon that he took straight out of the blood and thunder of the cheap London theater of which, as an impecunious youth, he was inordinately fond.

An example is seen in the language used by Bill Sykes, the murderer, in *Oliver Twist.* There is a scene, in which he is just going to do the murder—no, has just done it and is trying to escape. A child has got in the way and Sykes says to his associates, "Open the door of some place where I can lock this screeching hell babe . . ." Why he didn't "bump the child off," I forget just now. The present point is the language he used. He would have had just as good a phrase for bumping it.

Compare the *hell's accursed,* and the *foul fiend,* and such mild phrases. With objurations of that sort you sometimes couldn't tell whether the characters were cursing or praying; in fact in origin the two are one.

That reminds me of the language I once heard used by a man showing a "picture panorama"—the kind of thing they used to have long ago before the real "pictures" replaced it. In these pictures, when the successive scenes were shown, there was a man who did the talking. "Here you see this," and "now you see that . . ." and so on, as the scene went by. The man I speak of was showing a scene representing a Swiss peasant, getting swallowed up in a morass, or nearly swallowed up, till an angel appeared to save him. I was quite unable, and I still am, to distinguish whether the Swiss peasant and the angel were praying or swearing. In fact I don't think the picture man had thought it out. He took a chance.

His talk ran:

*Here you see the Swiss Alps. In the foreground is one of those dangerous more-asses, where the treacherous surface, with all the aspect of firm ground, offers no real support. Here you see a Swiss peasant. Look! He is stepping out on the more-ass. The ground yields beneath his feet. He moves forward more rapidly to escape. He begins to sink. He tries in vain to withdraw his feet. He is slowly sinking to his doom. Look, he lifts his hands and cries aloud: "Oh, Heaven," he says, "get me out of this more-ass. Oh, God, this is the damnedest more-ass. Christ! this is awful."*

*His prayer is heard. An angel appears, bending out from the clouds, her hand outstretched. "You poor soul," she says in a voice vibrating with pity. "You poor nut, you poor bastard . . . give me your hand, and come up." She takes him to her bosom, and he is saved.*

*So he would be, of course.*

. . . . . . .

But to turn back again to advice to writers. Don't think you can get away with swearing by putting something very close to it, something nearly as good and much cheaper, by a shift of a letter or two. Some writers try, for instance, to use "ruddy" to stand for "bloody." This is used especially in the mouths of English army sergeants and such. It is supposed to give a barrack-room touch. But it is really just a left-over piece of Victorian evasion. Rudyard Kipling used this trick, not so stale in his hey-day as it is now. One recalls his Soudanese negro Fuzzy-wuzzy, who was described as a "big, black, bounding beggar, who broke a British Square."

That's all right. Fuzzy-wuzzy was pretty close to that, but not just exactly that.

And here's another thing:

Don't try to get around the difficulty by turning the profanity into strokes (— — — —), or making it into asterisks (****). That's just feeble.

. . . . . . .

Asterisks and dots and strokes are hopeless. You can't *swear* with those things. They won't read right. . . . Read aloud, as they are, they would turn the pirate story into:

*"Three asterisks!" shouted the Pirate.*
*"Four," shouted the next.*
*"I'll make it six," yelled a third, adding a stroke and a colon.*

.    .    .    .    .    .    .

A person still young and inexperienced might think —surely there is no problem here. The true method would be to write down the very words that an actual person would actually use, to put the swearing in the book exactly as people swear it. But that, of course, would never do. Leaving out all question of whether the law allows it, art forbids it. It wouldn't sound right. Try it. Put down a set of foul, profane, obscene words—not samples, but the whole set used in what is called a string of profanity. It would sound awful for one paragraph, flat and stale after two, and beyond that utterly nauseating—in fact just like swearing. And you know how that sounds.

The only advice that can be given to the writer is, don't go further than others do. In fact, keep just a little behind them. If they say "guts," you say "bowels of compassion."

## CHAPTER VII

## HOW TO WRITE HISTORY

*Macaulay and his young ladies — College history;*
*Dust and lead — Writing an encyclopaedia; Your own*
*opinion we can do without — Picturesque history —*
*Francis Parkman floats down the Wisconsin River —*
*Alison executes Robespierre — A college history re-*
*moves Louis XVI; Now you see him, now you don't —*
*Overdone history writing — The close-nipped, tight-*
*lipped, underfed, overtaxed Americans at Valley Forge*
*— The interpretation of history — Which is history,*
*war or peace? — The People or the Powers?*

"I SHALL not be satisfied," said Macaulay, in reference
to the History of England which he proposed to write,
"unless I can produce something which shall for a few
days supersede the last fashionable novel on the tables
of young ladies." This is one of those unfortunate
statements which hang like millstones round their authors' necks. Macaulay's young ladies, clustering about
his chair to get a peep over his shoulder at what he
wrote, have obscured his reputation as a historian.
What Macaulay seems to be saying is that he will
bring down his history to the level of fashionable
young ladies. What he meant was that he would lift
the fashionable young ladies up to the level of history;
his history should be so well written that it would be
universal in its appeal. It proved so. Yet there grew

up gradually a contrast as between histories that aimed at brilliant and vivid presentation and those that aimed only at the accurate record of fact. The two are not incompatible but only special talent, in the highest reach only genius, could attain both ends. Macaulay could, and there are a few men, only a few, in both Britain and America who can do and are doing it to-day. It is the consistent endeavour of this book to avoid comparison and criticism of living authors and to avoid as far as possible any reference to their names. Otherwise one would wish here to indicate the eminence of such writers as Professor Morison and Mr. Woodward on our side of the water or of G. M. Trevelyan or the veteran Sir Charles Oman on the other. But I must not do so and pass them over in silence.

But the point is that there grew up since Macaulay's time, and especially with the increasing study of history as a college course, reckoned in majors, minors, passes and failures, an increasing contrast as between history of the literary type and history of the college type. The names do not entirely fit but let them pass for want of better. Here on the one side are Hume and Gibbon, Bancroft and Macaulay, Francis Parkman, John Richard Green, Goldwin Smith and the Trevelyans—*j'en passe et des meilleurs*. Here on the other are the rank and file of college historians writing books of fact, stating what happened for students to learn it, pass it and forget it. For the brilliant pages which the young ladies strained their necks to see, they substitute a history that is dull, arid and colourless, without light or character, without weather or scenery, without thrill or emotion, without life.

Worse still, the college textbook historians, by the sheer pride of their profession—or call it, if you like, by the academic Brahminism of college people, created and spread an impression that theirs was the real history. It is true that no young ladies ever peep over their shoulders, none but an unhappy First Year Girl all in tears because the Dean of Women has told her that she is "liable" to the French Revolution. That makes no difference. They regard the outside public as being only on the level of Macaulay himself.

Now here comes in a curious fact, and one which quite accidentally and wrongly seems to strengthen the claim of the dry-as-dust college history. Within the last half century opportunities and facilities for historical research, and the official encouragement given to it, have increased beyond belief. Carlyle, for example, breathed a sigh of regret that one could form no idea of the true shape and structure of the Bastille. Today we could give him a ground plan of the whole place. National archives are being as busily searched as grandfathers' trunks. Such records as those of what was once the *Bibliothèque Nationale* at Paris, or the archives of the Hudson's Bay Company, are what are called treasure houses of history. Hence each new book out-dates Macaulay by presenting new facts on William Penn, or renders Gibbon obsolete by resurrecting six pages of the personal diary of the Emperor Nero. Thus values get badly mixed. People confuse the material from which history is to be written, with the history itself. All the bricks ever baked in Babylon won't make Babylonian history—only the ingredients of the new loaf for the hand of the master baker to knead again to bread.

. . . . . . .

Thus stands what one may call the problem of writing history; or rather, one half of the problem for all that has been said concerns only the method of narration. There is still the problem of the interpretation of history. But let that sleep for the moment.

. . . . . . .

Now many people who wish to write might think that all this is no concern of theirs since they have not any aspirations towards writing history. To the majority of them a historian is a venerable old gentleman with a long white beard who is said to have spent twenty years in the British Museum and looks as if he had. His labour receives respect rather than envy. In all my college teaching days I have only known a few students who were born historians, who preferred fact to fancy and knew by instinct the difference between a first-hand document and a second-hand narrative. Such students took to history as ducks to water, and generally succeeded in it, as a labour of love is apt to do, returning to college twenty years after graduation, bearded and old, to receive a degree in recognition of what they had done towards a better knowledge of Ancient Crete or Early Babylon. Such labours are for the few.

But even the generality of writers are apt to find themselves concerned with history in the shape of historical romance, or stories with a historical setting, or in the plain matter of fact form of writing the condensed history required by an encyclopaedia and the

coloured history washed over tourist "literature."
Some notion of the presentation of historical problems
connected with history writing ought to be part of the
stock in trade and equipment of any literary worker.
These peculiar problems only appear when one meets
them in the attempt to write and studies them in actual cases and examples. Some history writing aims at
the presentation of facts without making any judgment
from them, as when an encyclopaedia includes the History of Portugal in 500 words. Other historical writing makes a presentation of facts with a view to proving a case, as when Macaulay writes an essay to put
Warren Hastings where he belongs. Some historical
writing on a larger canvas, the real history in the grand
sense, undertakes to convey the annals of a nation, or
even, of all the world at large. A lesser section of history relates curious and interesting facts for their own
sake, the story of the lost colony of Greenland, or the
fate of the expedition of Admiral Lapérouse.

Quite contrasted again is military history, itself a
whole province, aiming at the interest of the general
reader, but at times focussed to the narrower but technical viewpoint of the soldier student. Similarly there
branch away from the main trunk of history such expanding boughs as the history of commerce, of ex-
ploration, or the more newly discovered history of the
life of the people. Some of these branches are matched
by roots underground to be dug up as archaeology.
The weapon here is not the pen but the spade; and the
glowing page becomes the numbered catalogue. Centuries after the Greek historians and poets had done
with Troy, Dr. Heinrich Schliemann, in the eighties

of the last century, got after it with the spade. For many minds indeed there is higher interest in buried remains than in living actuality, more to them in a Roman helmet from Pompeii than in a modern Italian fedora hat. But let the fedora get old enough and it will rank with the helmet. This peculiar aspect of antiquity spreads wide till it extends from historians to coin collectors, and relic hunters and the midget pursuit of postage stamps.

But other branches of the great tree of history wave so high above the roots that they begin to take on something of the colours of the sky seen through the leaves. Here plays the fancy of the historical romance, and romantic history, better to vision thus enchanted than truth itself. Indeed this historical romance now extends its growth so fast and so far, that like the banyan tree it dips its branches to earth again, takes new roots and spreads on in a dozen varied forms. Here is first the pure romance of history, as written especially for children—nursery history—its pages bright with fluttering flags and flashing swords, or wet with tears that fell for the little princes in the Tower, or thumbed with eager interest where Horatius kept the bridge or some one else bridged the keep. Here is the historical novel of maximum specific gravity, as light as lead, sticking close to truth itself. Here again is the lighter historical novel turning all historical characters into such up-to-date individuals, all swearing and laughter and smut, that it makes them less convincing than ever. Beyond that history takes wings and flies up into the colours of the morning, just beautiful coloured patches done with gas in what is called "tourist literature" with sentences such as:

*Here Montcalm breathed his last, Wolfe having breathed his last first.*

.　　.　　.　　.　　.　　.　　.

Let us then, as an exercise proper to this volume, sit down to write history together. We will not attempt at first to strike the chords of romance but begin with the plain single notes of recorded fact. In other words we will begin by doing a history article for an encyclopaedia. Here we may well recall at the start the instructions sent out—it was years ago or I would not refer to it—by one of our leading encyclopaedias to its academic contributors, "This encyclopaedia wants the facts, and wants all the facts, but your own opinion we can do without." The language is as brutal as it is inelegant, but the editors were dealing with professors and had to take a firm stand. Yet even at that, many contributors to encyclopaedias take some time to learn and some never learn the difference between plain statements of fact and statements which seek to add life and colour. Facts, as such, for some reason or other, stand in deep disrepute with the ordinary mind. We speak of "bald" facts, a cruel comparison for elderly men to think of. Bald facts presumably need hair; dry facts need be made wet and dull facts to be brightened. Even when these epithets run out facts are described as plain, hard, unadorned, unwholesome—in short, fit company for no one. Yet the encyclopaedia lives on them as a raven grows wise on carrion.

We cannot wonder, therefore, that the literary spirit at first revolts from the harness of the encyclopaedia. But let us begin, anyway.

I suggest then that we undertake an article upon
Newfoundland. I suggest that subject because I recall
from some years back an article, or rather a contribution that never became an article, on Newfoundland
submitted to a great encyclopaedia at its own request
by an author so distinguished and so well acquainted
with Newfoundland that it seemed like asking Colum-
bus to write on America. That was the trouble. He
wrote too well and he knew too much. Indeed we
might start from the article thus submitted, as far as
I recall the text of it, instead of writing one of our
own. Of course my memory is inexact and blurred by
time, but it is correct enough for the essential idea.
The article begins:

*Newfoundland. This grand old isle, whose rocky
cliffs and granite coast bid defiance on one side to the
surges of the angry Atlantic, and on the other to the
treacherous ice, stands like a barrier thrown by jealous
Nature across the St. Lawrence, gateway to North
America.*

Stop! stop! That won't do at all. You can't call it
a *grand* old isle. Who said *grand?* That's just your
thought. Cut it out—and *isle*—you can't use that.
There's no such thing as isle in an encyclopaedia, only
an "island." Get down to bald fact; call it an island.
Better leave out old; keep that for the little section
called *palaeography* that we shall slip in later.

Very good. Now cut out all that "bidding defiance"
and angry Atlantic, etc. The Atlantic has never been
*angry* no more than the Pacific has been pacific—and
*surges*—leave them to the poets who can make a *surge*

suit; we can't. In fact wouldn't it be much nicer and more modest if we began:

*Newfoundland. An island in the North Atlantic (Lat. this, Long. that) lying across the opening of the St. Lawrence, its outer coast facing the Atlantic from northwest to south. The coast line deeply indented, is composed chiefly of basaltic rock overlying subcutaneous feldspar. . . .*

Now let our author continue for a while:

*Newfoundland is as old as, and older than, history. We cannot doubt that the Norsemen from Greenland came driving into its fiords on the foam of the east wind. John Cabot, we know, gazed at its iron-bound shores from the deck of his caravel. For half a century the swarthy Basque fisherman gathered its prolific cod to feed a fasting Christendom. But the banner of England was first proudly hoisted on its soil by the chivalrous Sir Humphrey Gilbert and his dare-devil Elizabethan crew fresh from their destruction of the Armada.*

Stop! stop! It's all gone wrong again. The Norsemen didn't *drive in on the foam.* The proper phrase is, *visited the coast.* John Cabot didn't *gaze* at it. He saw it. Get back to hard fact—and he may have been on the deck of his caravel or sitting up on the main truck —see under *Ships; Yards; Rigging.* And the Basque fishermen. It's quite right to refer to them. They came back and forward for a century. But you mustn't call them *swarthy,* at least not here; this is no place for saying that the Basques are swarthy. That information belongs elsewhere, under *Races of Europe, Human Complexion,* see also *Dermatology* and disease of the skin. And never mind what cod are used for—that's another matter . . . and of course the banner was really hoisted *proudly* but we mustn't say so; and, of course, the Elizabethan sailors should not have been called dare-devils but simply labelled see under *Armada.*

Which shows one of the peculiar technical difficulties in writing for an encyclopaedia—how to know what belongs in your own article and what belongs elsewhere. An untrained writer wanders like a cow on the roadside. The editor has to cut out his material and insert, see under *Cod Fisheries,* see under *Gilbert,* see *Strait.* But the technical man keeps inside the fence, or even gets out of difficulties when he fails to find information by passing the buck with a see under *something else.* Thus: *The aborigines of Newfoundland, now dead, were of mixed origin* (see under *North American Indians*).

But this is a purely technical matter, more of editorial than literary interest. We may let it go at that.

For if I remember rightly it was at about this point of editorial revision that the distinguished author withdrew his article. It was published later, at about five times encyclopaedia prices, with beautiful illustrations by the *Ladies' Something Magazine* under the title *O! Cod.*

. . . . . . .

Now many people who want to write might think that this business of encyclopaedia writing and the method of encyclopaedia statement is of no interest or advantage to people who are interested only in the idea of writing stories. There they are quite wrong. In relating a story, which is from the nature of the case untrue, one of the chief problems is how to make it sound true. This gift of producing "verisimilitude" (likeness to truth), as we saw in the last chapter, is a very high literary art, often instinctive and unconscious, but capable like all other instinctive performances of improvement by industry.

Perhaps I have not made sufficiently clear what I mean by the difference between an encyclopaedia sentence and a literary sentence. The literary sentence may often be superior in reach, but it doesn't sound quite as true. . . . Example: We are writing a sea story and we want to show what a terrific fellow the bosun was.

*Literary method:*

*I do not think I have ever seen anyone who gave me the same impression of elemental power as the bosun.*

*Encyclopaedia method:*

*The bosun was a gigantic man, swarthy and heavily set, six feet two by 50 inches.* One description says what the bosun *was,* the other tells what we think about the bosun. Both ways of writing are quite in order. But there are times when the encyclopaedia style creates the better effect.

. . . . . . .

But let us pass from this outlying ground to the main field of history, the writing of the annals of a nation, the thing that anyone tries to do who writes a book called the *History of the United States,* or the

*History of England.* This is the real thing and from
the days of Thucydides and Tacitus it has called forth
much of the best intellectual power of mankind. Many
people never tire of history. Indeed our life interest in
literature begins with it in infancy since Jack the Giant
Killer, as narrated, is straight history. "Once upon a
time"—begins the mother, in opening the narration,
and the charm of the old phrase lingers on for ever.

. . . . . . .

Now the principal thing that I want to say here is
that real history, as apart from mere books of material, cannot be presented so as to convey the full and
adequate impression of what happened without a fitting presentation of scene and circumstance. History
in other words must be "literary." This is the point
which I indicated above and which I now wish to elaborate with practical examples.

Let us consider, as the most striking case in point,
the work of Francis Parkman. Parkman lived from
1823 to 1893. He wrote a dozen volumes dealing with
the history of North America from the beginning of
European settlement until the fall of the French Empire on this continent. The series practically ends with
*Montcalm and Wolfe* since the *Conspiracy of Pontiac,*
the Indian war that followed the surrender of New
France, in 1760 and the Cession of 1763, was merely
an appendage of what went before. Parkman worked
with a zeal that never slackened and an industry that
never flagged, visited battlefields, delved into archives,
yet with the resulting product of a page so clear and
lucid and attractive, so easy to read, so effortless to
remember, that many of his readers never think him a

historian at all. They think he was only a writer. You
see, what he wrote is such easy stuff that you could
hardly call it history.

Parkman has an intense and instinctive feeling for
the presentation of each event in the light of the scene
and surroundings. He must know not only what happened but what it was like where it happened. The
statement that Cain killed Abel would be of little use
to him. He must know whether it was at midnight in
a thunderstorm in the heart of a forest, or in the still
dawn of a summer morning just as the mist rose off
the Garden of Eden. For others it is quite enough that
Cain killed Abel; for a lawyer, for instance, anything
else is extraneous. He would object to bringing in the
weather as evidence. Many writers of history take it in
just this sense. They would digest Parkman's volumes
into a quarter of their size and there would be nothing
left of them.

For Parkman's pages are redolent of the salt wind
off the sea and the odor of the forest; they burn with
the glare of the sun on the desert sand and are still and
cool with the mist of the morning; they are swept with
the wind over the prairies where the "dark hollows
seem to glide along and chase the sunny ridges."

Look through the pages of Parkman's books and
you will find an unending series of magic phrases of
scene and sky.

Or take a sustained passage and observe the cumula-
tive effect, the intensity of the reality. Here, in the volume *La Salle and the Discovery of the Great West,*
are Joliet and Marquette (1673) at the Wisconsin
River. They have passed from Lake Michigan up the
river and over the marshes and have now reached

waters moving the other way, to bear them to the Mississippi.

*Carrying their canoes a mile and a half over the prairie and through the marsh, they launched them upon the Wisconsin, bade farewell to the waters that flowed to the St. Lawrence, and committed themselves to the current that was to bear them they knew not whither—perhaps to the Gulf of Mexico, perhaps to the South Sea or the Gulf of California. They glided calmly down the tranquil stream, by islands choked with trees and matted with entangling grape-vines; by forests, groves, and prairies, the parks and pleasure grounds of a prodigal nature; by thickets and marshes and broad bare sand-bars under the shadowing trees between whose tops looked down from afar the bold brow of some wooded bluff. At night, the bivouac— the canoes inverted on the bank, the flickering fire, the meal of bison flesh or venison, the evening pipes and slumber beneath the stars; and when in the morning they embarked again, the mist hung on the river like a bridal veil, then melted before the sun, till the glassy water and the languid woods basked breathless in the sultry glare.*

.        .        .        .        .        .        .

It may be objected, of course, that this beautiful imagery, this completed picture, demands time and space. There is not room for it within an ordinary history book. This is quite true. But it means that the writer of any history book, short or long, should contrive to get as much of this effect as the space will allow, should feel that there is a certain indispensable minimum of it that must be there or the book is not history. There is no hardship in telling a writer to sacrifice a certain amount of detail of fact for a greater intensity of presentation. After all, details are infinite. When you have given all you can give there are plenty more behind.

. . . . . . .

On the other hand historians determined to insert every last detail of fact, every first and last cause, so crowd and condense their material as to defeat their own end. What they write becomes unintelligible without a special effort, and unrememberable even with one.

The extreme type of this kind of writing is found in what are sometimes called in their titles "political" histories of this or that country. This means that they not only leave out the weather, but every other human or natural aspect of everything except meetings, votes, motions, committees, resolutions and sentences of execution. The effect is dreary beyond words. One such history of modern Europe written in French but translated into English words, was inflicted so long and so cruelly on so many of our American universities that it is better not to name it. But we may throw against the glass houses of our neighbours the bricks that we wouldn't throw into our own, and refer to another modern French work, Aulard's *Histoire Politique de la Révolution Française*. In this the Assembly meets, calls itself to the order of the day, calls itself out of the order of the day, goes into a committee and comes right out of it, expels itself, meets outside, votes death, abrogates the vote, declares the constitution open, then closed—the whole thing punctuated by public executions without wind or weather or scenery or spectators—and that is called the French Revolution.

One admits, of course, the need for tabulated fact. But such a thing is only like a guide book or a street directory. Let it be granted, of course, that there is a certain necessary apparatus of dates and names indispensable to history as a frame to hold itself in. But dates are not history, only a necessary adjunct but no more history than a pair of braces is a pair of trousers. The dates hold the history up. But a man with a list of dates only makes as sorry a showing as a man with braces but no trousers.

.    .    .    .    .    .    .

Speaking still of the French Revolution we may realize that the great moments of the world's history can only be properly appreciated when properly presented. Here are two contrasted pictures from the history of the French Revolution. The first is Sir Archibald Alison's account (*History of Europe*) of the execution of Robespierre. The next is the execution of Louis XVI as carried out in a college history.

Here is Alison:

"At four in the afternoon all Paris was in motion to witness the death of the tyrant. He was placed on the chariot, between Henriot and Couthon, whose persons were as mutilated as his own, the last in the vehicle, in order that, with the usual barbarity of the period, which he himself had been instrumental in introducing, he should see all his friends perish before him. They were bound by ropes to the benches of the car in which they were seated; and the rolling of the vehicle during the long passage, which was through the most populous quarters of Paris, produced such pain in their wounds that they at times screamed aloud. The gendarmes rode with their sabres presented to the people who clapped their hands, as they had done when Danton was led to execution. Robespierre's forehead, one eye, and part of the cheek, were alone seen above the bandage which bound up the broken jaw. St. Just evinced through-out the most unconquerable fortitude. Robespierre cast his eyes on the crowd, turned them aside, and shrugged his shoulders. The multitude, which for long had ceased to attend the executions, manifested the utmost joy at their fate. They were conducted to the Place de la Revolution; the scaffold was placed on the spot where Louis XVI and Marie Antoinette had suffered. The Statue of Liberty still surmounted the scene. Never had such a crowd been witnessed on any former occasion; the streets, despite the earliness of the hour, were thronged to excess; every window was filled; even the roofs of the houses, like the manned yards of a ship, were crowded with spectators. The joy was universal; it almost approached to delirium. The blood from Robespierre's jaw burst through the bandage, and overflowed his dress; his face was ghastly pale. He kept his eyes shut, when he saw the general feeling, during the time the procession lasted, but could not close his ears against the imprecations of the multitude. A woman, breaking from the crowd, exclaimed— 'Murderer of all my kindred! Your agony fills me with joy; descend to hell covered with the curses of every mother in France!' He ascended the scaffold with a firm step, and was laid down near the axe.

Twenty of his comrades were executed before him; during the time they were suffering, he lay on the scaffold with his eyes shut, never uttering a word. When lifted up to be tied to the fatal plank, the executioner tore the bandage from his face; the lower jaw fell upon his breast, and he uttered a yell which filled every heart with horror. For some minutes the frightful figure was held up, fixed to the board, to the multitude; he was then placed under the axe, and the last sounds which reached his ears were the exulting shouts, which were prolonged for some minutes after his death."

Here on the other hand is the way in which King Louis XVI is executed in a modern compendium history, which many will recognize without my naming it.

"*On the morning of the 21st he was driven in the company of Santerre and Garat to the Place de la Revolution.*"

This sounds like a civic reception.

"*Although the attitude of the crowd was on the whole sympathetic, the Jacobins managed everything so well that no incident occurred.*"

None, that is, except cutting off the King's head.

"*Louis' behaviour on the scaffold was marked by perfect composure and piety. His attempt to address the crowd was cut short by the roll of drums.*"

It is not mentioned that the King's head was cut off. But the account adds that *at 10:20 A.M. on Jan. 21, 1793, his head was held up to the crowd by Sanson the executioner.* Somebody must have cut it off a little before that.

No doubt the writer of this account would say that everything essential is there. Yet to some people it seems—it may be said without ill-nature—a little too comfortable. It suggests an odd mixture of a civic function and a scene of horror—perhaps it was. One might still without ill-nature, offer a comparison with a similar mixed scene in that good old book of Max Adeler' called *Out of the Hurly-Burly*. Here the mixture arise from a country newspaper getting the type of two articles mixed—one an account of a presentation gift to the Rev. Dr. Hopkins and the other a description o a new hog-killing machine.

*"Several of the Rev. Dr. Hopkins's friends called upon him yesterday, and after a brief conversation the unsuspecting hog was seized by the hind legs and slid along a beam until he reached the hot-water tank His friends explained the object of their visit and presented to him a very handsome butcher who grabbed him by his tail, swung him around, slit his throat from ear to ear, and in less than a minute the carcass was i the water."*

. . . . . . .

The unhappy Louis XVI had nothing on the Rev Dr. Hopkins. But perhaps the analogy is far-fetched or fetched for the sake of fetching it. It may be pardoned; history is dull stuff anyway and needs brightening up with Dr. Hopkins.

Let it be agreed, of course, that in this writing o history the picturesque aspect must be kept within it proper limits. It must never run to picturesqueness fo picturesqueness's sake. Making pictures is one thing writing history is another. There was a famous French romanticist who saw and described Niagara Falls while still the country was wilderness. He puts in all the foam, mist, noise, roar, trees, wind—even the wild monkeys dangling from the trees—he says so. Parkman would have given the Falls two lines, and yet caught the sound of them, and assigned the monkeys to a footnote. Similarly William Cullen Bryant describes the prairies and covers a thousand lines. Parkman spreads them noiselessly out underfoot for the explorer Vérendrye and those who followed. In the one treatment the picturesque is a picture and the history a background to muse upon; in the other the picturesque element is introduced only to obtain the full comprehension of the narrative, impossible without it. Here for instance is the English historian John Richard Green—(*Short History of the English People*), a master of condensed and vivid imagery—describing the effect of the preaching of the first Methodists to the working people of England. *Their voice was soon heard in the wildest and most barbarous corners of the land, among the bleak moors of Northumberland, or in the dens of London, or in the long galleries where in the pauses of his labour the Cornish miner listens to the sobbing of the sea.* When I read that as a boy at school I thought it wonderful and I think so still. Nor can you get the same effect of reality by writing after the compendium fashion:

*Whitefield then went to the West of England where he preached at Taunton (Sept. 3), at Exmouth (Sept. 4), at Wrexmouth (Sept. 5), and at Pargelly, Clovelly, and Pingelly on three following days. On*

*some of these occasions Mr. Whitefield preached un-*
*derground, once at a mean barometic altitude (or lack*
*of it) 100 feet below sea-level.*

This will never convey what is needed.

. . . . . .

On the other hand the attempt to make history
vivid, if overdone and underdone by those who can't do
it, produces mere bombast, a potful of words and epithets, stock phrases, and forced comparisons. With
such writers the Mississippi is always *The Father of*
*Waters,* the Saskatchewan the *mighty Saskatchewan.*
The rivers always roll, the mountains frown, the precipices yawn—certainly one can't blame the precipices.
The colour is so thick, so continuous, that the reader
longs for a plain statement, such as, *Washington re-*
*mained with his army at Valley Forge from the first*
*of the month till the fifteenth,* and not,

*Here remained the intrepid, unbudging, unbudge-*
*able Washington, his back against the frozen snow-*
*drifts in which were firmly set his hard-bitten, close-*
*nipped, underfed, overtaxed Americans, still waving*
*the Stars and Stripes.*

This type of writing is often called journalese but
there is a distinction. The journalist writes it only to
give the people what the people want, as you give
sugar candy to children; he really knows better. But
the bombast historian is trying his best to show the
people what they ought to want.

. . . . . .

One further word needs to be said to distinguish
between the problem of how to write history and the

problem of how to interpret it. It is with the first of
these, the art of narration, that this present book is
properly concerned. The other problem, commonly
called the philosophy of history, belongs elsewhere.
It deals with such matters as to whether history repeats itself, in other words whether in some degree the
study of history has a prophetic character and helps
us to foretell the future. The idea of general historical laws has found great favour in the past, especially
as it could go hand in hand with a divine or theologi-
cal interpretation. But in our complicated and changing
events it is impossible to trace the effect of such general laws and nothing can be prophesied till it is over.
General laws are thus out of date. But particular se-
quences of history are still capable of discussion, and
indeed call for it. Did the French Revolution make
Europe or ruin it? Such questions are to most of us
more engrossing than the lesser problem of how to
narrate what happened in the French Revolution. But
writing the Revolution must come first and interpret-
ing it after.

   .     .     .     .     .     .     .

There is also the question of "selecting" history—
which is a part of its interpretation. Is history to be a
record of monarchs and dynasties, or "good Kings"
and "bad Kings," as it used to be in the English school-
book *Little Arthur's England?* Is it mainly a record of
wars, battles, conquests and cessions of territory, the
drum-and-fife history which was the prevailing type
of a century ago? On the other hand history can be
thought of as the story of the life of a people—the
plain people, all the people—and of the rise of indus-

try and the progress of agricultural settlement—a sort of Farmers' Almanac in place of a Court Circular.

. . . . . . .

Now some people, as notably Thomas Carlyle, have thought that the plain people are always led, moulded and made or marred in their destiny by the people of exception, good and bad—for England, let us say the Oliver Cromwells and the Charles Wesleys and the Cecil Rhodeses. Hence even if you pin your history down to the plain people it won't stay there. This theory, along with the regal theory, fell flatter and flatter in Victorian times, during the Great Peace of 1815-1854, that was to last forever, and even in the Victorian half century that followed when war seemed forever ended for the home people of Great Britain and henceforth only an intermittent thing of exception, for savages, foreign revolutionaries and such. Hence the British historians more and more laid stress on the history of the people. They no longer wanted the children to read of the conflict of the Wars of the Roses, of the battles over in the snows of Towton and King Richard shouting for a horse at Bosworth Field. They wanted them to learn all about the life of the people, how the Britons painted themselves blue and the Normans made tapestry and the minstrels sang in the land. How much of these pictures really got home it is hard to say. The battles were simpler for children to understand and to imitate. The life in the castle beat them. I recall a school-paper answer in a juvenile class in my teaching days, given to an examination question about life in the castle. "In the evening in the Great Hall," wrote the pupil, "the men used to get drunk and play chess." It was a high compliment to British character but looks poor as an encouragement to historical method.

John Richard Green of the *Short History* was the most ardent advocate of this school. "War plays a small part," he writes, "in the real story of European nations, and in that of England its part is smaller than in any." Yet Sir Charles Oman, the veteran historian of the art of war, looking back from 1941 in a retrospect of the half a century since Green wrote, remarked, "What a pity Green did not live to see 1914, or 1939!" Green, as Oman points out, and plenty of others of his day, had a comfortable sort of democratic, evolutionary idea of history, in which "freedom had broadened down from precedent to precedent." Great men counted for relatively little. The worst was over. There were just a few little things, such as the slums, poverty and unemployment left to attend to. Meantime, history could be made of druids and mistletoe, tapestry, Elizabethan sheep-runs (instead of the execution of Mary Queen of Scots), spinning-machines, instead of the American revolution, and gas light and steam print instead of Waterloo.

.    .    .    .    .    .    .

Yet after all if war is to be the chief history, all the greater curse on it.

.    .    .    .    .    .    .

It is a fascinating and interesting inquiry, greatly commended to all who write, or read.

## CHAPTER VIII

## HOW TO WRITE HISTORICAL NOVELS

*The charm of the past — Saxon oak trees and Norman courtyards — Difficulty to make it live — Difference (if any) between Tennyson's King Arthur and a stuffed shirt — Antiquarian affectation — Don't say the knight wore a salade — How to make historic people talk — Include me out, laughed Mary Queen of Scots — Lady Rowena at the bat — The beam in our own eye — Dirt enough to attract clean minds — Private life of Peter the Hermit*

BUT now we come to the real thing, the one most connected for our purpose with history—the writing of historical fiction. There is a never-ending attraction in the past. For the past contains the good old times, and also the bad old times. Our phrases cluster round it as the "days of old," and the "men of old," and beyond these again "the days of yore." Here, as everywhere, the individual repeats the experience of the race. He looks back to the prehistoric twilight of the nursery, the cave-man days of the boyhood farm, the heroes of high school; he carries the same viewpoint of his own life as a nation does of its centuries, with all the colours of the early morning, when the woods were green and the sky always blue and love beautiful and sweet.

* * * * * * * *

Well may a child or boy of imaginative mind slip out of the pages of a school book into dreams of Saxon England, of men riding under the great oak trees . . . of Norman knights clattering on the pavement of the courtyard . . . and most of all, of the long ships with beaks like dragons, driving on to the beaches of England under a huge square sail and with that forever the mystery and magic of the sea.

So the interest comes to him—the *urge* people often call it now but the word sounds too much like *itch*—so shall we say the *impulse,* to write it all down, reproduce the scenes and people that pass like a bannered procession before his inner vision. He tries to do so—with a pitiable result . . . all that comes from his pen is "How now," said Sir Boris, leaping in full armour from his horse and drawing his double-edged sword as he came down, "foul catiff, woulds't insult a lady! Have at you. Here's one on you!" The pen hesitates, stops. Would Sir Boris really talk like that? Would he or any one really say, *Have at you!* Could he really leap with all that iron stuff? It would give his heels an awful jolt. The pen drops . . . but another boy picks it up and the eternal struggle goes on, to reproduce the past. Has it ever succeeded? Some people think it never can. We can make something else, or something better, or something just as good—but not the past. There is, as it were, a contradiction in terms; because it is past we cannot make it present.

. . . . . . .

Some critics, we say, have said that a real historical novel is once and for all an impossibility . . . What seems to one generation a vivid picture of the past seems to the next as unnatural as a stiff shirt. The heroic turns to the comic . . . Many people, and I am one, think Tennyson's knights very funny people. But perhaps we can create a dream world of the past if we cannot make a real one . . . make something which is better than reality . . . since actual life is poor stuff anyway. . . . Indeed it is only recently—in the larger sense—that the idea of portraying life-as-it-is became the ideal of literature. The earlier idea was of life better than it is.

It is into these perplexities and difficulties and contradictions that we wish to inquire, that anyone may well inquire who wishes to write stories of the past.

. . . . . . .

Historical fiction began in earnest for Britain and America with the novels of Sir Walter Scott. . . . The success and acclaim were immediate. . . . It is said that when *Waverley* appeared people stopped one another, book in hand, on the streets of Edinburgh, to ask "Have you read it?" Yet *Waverley* was in a sense scarcely historic to the people who first read it. Its second title, *'Tis Sixty Years Since,* shows it merely in the retrospect of a vanishing horizon, that verge of the present retreating into the past, that is history to the young and yesterday to the old, yet near to both. Scott reached back to the Middle Ages and the Crusades—the real thing—with *Ivanhoe* and the *Talisman,* then for the most part confined himself to the romance of Scotland.

With Scott began the weaving of the unending web of historic fiction, which at times slackened, waxed or waned but has never stopped. Washington Irving followed with the picture past of *Father Knickerbocker* in New York and *Rip Van Winkle* in the hills of the Hudson, seen, as it were, through tobacco smoke. Fenimore Cooper in Indian feathers crawled through the underbrush, not snapping a single twig and all Europe crawled, breathless or breathing hard, behind him. Charles Dickens wrote of today. To him the past was as rotten as it was to Mark Twain. Once—it was after reading Carlyle's *French Revolution*—he reached back towards the past in his *Tale of Two Cities,* and made a better French Revolution than the real one. But after all the Revolution was still a thing of yesterday. In *Barnaby Rudge* Dickens reached a little back to the Lord George Gordon Riots of 1781. But this is not history writing, since in unchanging England Mr. Willett's Maypole Inn and all that went with love and locksmiths, was still there when Dickens wrote. Dickens, indeed stuck to today (his day) and moved along with it. When the railway train came in he saw at once the "romance" of it and used it to kill one of his villains under its headlights.

But other writers moved backwards. Thackeray revived colonial America. Harrison Ainsworth contrived a bloody mixture of towers and dungeons, blocks and axes which would be terrifying if it weren't tedious. One of his sentences is four feet long. Then came Bulwer-Lytton, most historical of all, and all the world walked the colonnaded porticoes and tessellated pavements of ancient Rome, groped their way with Lydia, the blind girl, and sought shelter in vain from the black destruction that overwhelmed Pompeii.

The current never stopped. Boys walked the Saxon

forest and sailed the Spanish Main with Charles Kingsley. Such a writer as the late Mr. Henty turned history stories to mass production, adapting every epoch of the world for reading under a school desk during classes. In *Ben Hur* General Wallace, a Civil War veteran, whirled in furious chariots around the Roman arena and in *Quo Vadis?* Henryk Sienkiewicz asked the world again the agelong question, "Whither goest thou?" and lifted the curtain on the inspired days of Christianity in Rome. The turn of the century for a time witnessed feudalism in a flood. Then came the adjunct of the moving picture with its marvellous power of instantaneous presentation to the eye of scenes hitherto produced word by word to the ear. Whether it obliterates or stimulates imagination no one yet knows.

The moving picture should have killed the historical novel. It didn't. It only made it longer—and made success more rapid, wider and more evanescent—the best seller withers like the grass on the prairies; the old books remain like the mountains on the horizon; not as being better but as made when the world was young. But the historical novel, influenced by the moving picture as the induced currents flow in parallel wires, changed its scope. It has stepped out, so to speak; no longer wants to be decorous and ponderous and dignified but must have its characters up-to-date, so real, as we said above, that they are unreal, so much alive that they seem galvanized rather than living, and with just enough nastiness in it to attract clean-minded people.

.    .    .    .    .    .    .

The first advice always given to people who wish to write historical stories is that they must read history. This is obviously true in a sense. But they must be careful. They are told that they must saturate themselves, soak themselves, so to speak, in the period. This is all right as long as they retain the power to distinguish between what is interesting in itself and what is interesting only to an antiquarian. Now writers who make studies for historical novels, studies of ancient manners, customs, armour, etc. etc., are apt to become affected by what is called an antiquarian interest. This is quite harmless within a moderate degree, though always tiresome at a dinner party. Take the question of armour. The people of the Middle Ages used lots of it and each piece of it had a different name. Only a few, such as *helmet* and *breastplate,* have any meaning now. But some knights wore a light *salade* in place of a helmet. Think what a temptation for a historical writer to say, *With these final words Ugo Negroli closed down his salade and strode away.*

A writer of the old style, of the days of Scott, would have been allowed a footnote to say, *"The salade, or sallet, a light flexible helmet, was first worn in the fifteenth century and is said to have been invented by the Negroli family."* A knight in full armour in that century, after having put on the clothes which we call his shirt and his pants and socks, put on twenty-three pieces of what Mark Twain's Yankee called *hardware.* They included such things as a *ventail* and *rondel,* a *gorget,* a *rerebrace* (one can imagine its use), a *tacet,* a pair of *greaves,* and finally a pair of *sollerets* laced round his feet—by some one else, as the knight was now completely immobilized. What a temptation then for a writer who has soaked himself in the fascinating study of armour to write, *Sir Tancred the Two-Spot stood before the steel mirror adjusting his ventail, having already fastened his vambrace and his loin guard, screwed down his kneecops and passed the bolts through his rerebrace.* Historical fiction is much disfigured with this stuff, written by writers who either know too much or too little. Any writer of today should be warned against this temptation. Don't use queer words just because you know them. After all this list of queer bits of costume is nothing more in itself than any other list, let us say than a laundry list of today, *pyjamas, combinations, dickies, etc.* Let the knight put on those. As with armour, so with arms. There is no sense in giving to things familiar to us as swords and shields, javelins and battle-axes the foreign names used by the foreign people engaged in the fight. Very often it obscures rather than illuminates the combat. Under this pedantic treatment the description of a single combat in Roman times appears as follows— more or less:

*The legionary stood his ground fearlessly against the huge figure of the advancing Gaul, who had leaped from arch to arch of the broken bridge and now stood beside him on the hither bank of the river. Marcus gave way not an inch but drawing his straight flat* ENSIS *from its* POCULUM *he directed a furious thrust straight at the hardened leather* PABULUM *of his gigantic adversary. The Gaul caught the blow deftly on his wooden* CEREBELLUM *and with a shout of de-*

*fiance hurled his native* CUSPIDOR *full at the* STERNUM *of the Roman; the legionary deftly stepped aside to avoid the flying* CUSPIDOR *while in his return his own* AZALEA *reached home between the joints of the Gaul. . . . The Gaul, maddened with pain, now swung aloft his double-headed axis, a weapon resembling a double-headed axe, and was about to rush in to close quarters. But at this moment loud cries arose from the wood. A furious* AURIGA *came hurtling from out the trees followed by the glittering* HASTAE *of a* COHORS. *The Gaul hesitated, lowered his weapon, turned, and with a shout of defiance cleared the* FLUMEN *at a single bound and disappeared into the* SILVA.

This is a fine description but more appreciated if it is understood that an *auriga* is not a dragon-fly and that *hastae* are not insects.

． ． ． ． ． ． ．

But the difficulty of finding ways and means of description—suitable words—in historical novels is as nothing compared with the difficulty that arises when the characters open their mouths to speak. These historical people belong to all ages and countries from the ancient Egypt of four thousand years back, down the centuries and in and out among the Empires. How then are they to speak? Obviously they have got to talk English since nothing else would be understood. But it can't be the actual English of today, the colloquial talk of the hour, for that would sound hopelessly artificial. Some writers try it, but it simply won't work. The result is like this:

"How are you today, old bean?" said the Roman praetor.

.　　.　　.　　.　　.　　.　　.

"What a darned nuisance!" said the Queen of Sheba.

.　　.　　.　　.　　.　　.

"Include me out!" laughed Mary Queen of Scots.

.　　.　　.　　.　　.　　.

"Hurry up, boys, finish your booze!" called King Arthur across the Round Table.

.　　.　　.　　.　　.　　.

No, they didn't, they couldn't have said that. At least that's exactly what they did say but it doesn't sound right. King Arthur must be made to say "Drain me your goblets, Sir Knights, and to horse!"

That last touch is exactly the kind of queer conventional English that has grown up as the special jargon of the historical novel. It is made up partly of old spelling—like *'tis* for *it's*, which really sound the same. Compare *It is a long way*, with *'Tis a long way*, and *it's a long way*, and you will find they all amount to *s'long way*. But the historical novel people all say *'Tis*, just as they all say *Will ye*, though it sounds exactly the same as our ordinary *Will you*. With this goes a set of half old, half new words and a special set of swearing. It is really one of the forms of broken English like the pigeon English of business China, and the lingo of the West African Coast.

.　　.　　.　　.　　.　　.

All these forms of broken English, created out of necessity, are based on one and the same plan of taking a few words and phrases and working them overtime to fit all sorts of meaning. Pigeon English—it means business English—uses constantly *A.1.* and *top-side* and the word *pigeon* (business) itself. In pigeon English a *professor emeritus* is called an *A.1. top-side word-pigeon man.* The West African lingo uses a few phrases like *lib'* (*live for*), *belong him, one piece,* etc., where we use adjectives. Thus in West Africa a "venerable statesman" becomes *Big fellow lib' for talk no hair belong him.*

The conventional language of historical novels has similarly gathered up its stock-in-trade a lot of conventional phrases and half obsolete words worn with use—such words as *sore* and *fain* and *right,* etc. *In sooth I was right weary with walking and would fain have slept but was sore afraid to do so,* etc. These phrases, coupled with *'Tis's* and *Ye's,* old bad spelling and manufactured profanity, serve as English for historical purposes.

.     .     .     .     .     .     .

It is hard to see how to remedy it. Let us turn back again to Walter Scott who first opened the road and gave the succeeding generations what was either a lead or a misleading turn. Here is Scott about to write *Ivanhoe* and the *Talisman,* stories of the days of Richard Coeur de Lion (1189-1199) and his regent brother Prince John. Now the people chiefly concerned are Norman knights and ladies. How are they to talk? What they really spoke was the Norman French of the day, very much like modern French, but not enough so to be understood by a Frenchman of today, any more than we could understand the English

of a peasant in East Anglia of 1189. No people of
class spoke English in England for a hundred years
after King John. How, we repeat, shall they be made
to talk? Not in Norman French for the reader
wouldn't understand it and Scott couldn't write it. They
must talk in English, but yet not too much like the
English of today or it would sound unnatural. Hence
they talk in a sort of older English with plenty of half-
lost words, a pure convention, without an atom of
logic to it.

"If I have offended," said Sir Brian, "I crave your
pardon."

It is not possible for Sir Brian to say, "I'm sorry,
boys" which is the real equivalent of his Norman
French.

"A truce with your railing, Sir Knights," said
FitzUrse.

What FitzUrse really said in Norman French was
equal to, *Quit fooling, fellers*—but again that is impossible.

Such is the pace that was set and the pattern that
was traced. The tissue of language was shot with various oaths and exclamations, which are correct in a
sense that no doubt somebody used them sometimes,
but incorrect in that they leave out other ones that
many people used much of the time. They are selected
as foul language because they have dried out so long
that there was no offense in them. Those that still kept
their meaning, like the much-used "bloody" are ruled
out as foul language because still foul. If FitzUrse had
exclaimed *What the bloody hell!* Scott's readers would
have fallen off their stools.

This point of how to use bad language in literature is, however, a special matter to be treated later. Here we can only indicate some of the oaths, abjurations and exclamations which Scott and his successors fished out of the backwaters of Norman and Medieval England.

For the use of lords, knights and military men generally: *morbleu, parsambleu! Zounds!* (God's wounds) *Oddsbodekins!* etc. For the use of noble ladies: *oddspitikins* (for the sake of God's pity). For Kings themselves: *By the splendour of God* (King Richard); *By God's teeth!* (King John).

Apart from the choice of words Scott had to face the problem, passed on to all his successors until today, as to how well exalted characters are to talk and what is the kind of language a beautiful woman must use. His general decision was that the more exalted a character the more exalted his speech, and that for a noble and beautiful female no language could be too good, no rhetoric too elegant. The system reaches its climax when the Lady Rowena opens her mouth. She was, it will be remembered by readers of *Ivanhoe,* a heroine who had been abducted by Maurice de Bracy, a villain.

. . . . . . .

"Alas! fair Rowena!" returned De Bracy, "you are in the presence of your captive, not your jailer; and it is from your fair eyes that De Bracy must receive that doom which you fondly expect from him."

"I know you not, sir," said the lady, drawing herself up with all the pride of offended rank and beauty, "I know you not—and the insolent familiarity with which you apply to me the jargon of a troubadour, forms no apology for the violence of a robber."

Pretty neat language to use offhand! And Lady Rowena follows it up with sentence after sentence as knock-out blows against De Bracy. She meets him at every point. De Bracy—who can blame him?—gets a little impatient.

"Courtesy of tongue"—Rowena comes back at him, "when it is used to veil churlishness of deed, is but a knight's girdle around the breast of a base clown. I wonder not that the restraint appears to gall you— more it were for your honour to have retained the dress and the language of an outlaw than to veil the deeds of one under an affectation of gentle language and demeanour."

This language of rhetoric and repartee comes with the utmost ease to Lady Rowena. She never has to fumble and put in, "I mean to say," or "do you see," or anything like that. Her mind moves too fast. We have some pretty nimble intelligences among us, especially the people who carry on the radio quizzes, but I doubt if even Professor Billy Phelps or Franklin P. Adams could keep up with the Lady Rowena. I don't know of any living person who could take her on, except perhaps Charlie McCarthy.

The fact is that there never were in the world such two people as De Bracy and the Lady Rowena. They are not real life. They are meant, as we said, to be better than real.

.　　.　　.　　.　　.　　.　　.

The latest form and fashion of historical novel is based on the presentation of the great people. The conspicuous people of past history. They are all taken in turn. The professional writer reflects—"Let me see

—Peter the Hermit, who was he? I wonder if he has been written up" . . . and within a few months the reviewers are writing: *Mr. Snide's new Peter the Hermit (pp. 1030) is an arresting book, giving an entirely different view from that usually held of the personal character of the man who summoned Europe to the First Crusade. It appears that Peter was far from being the Hermit commonly supposed. Mr. Snide traces his various amours, some of a character scarcely to bear decent repetition (it is all Mr. Snide can do). Mr. Snide shows also that his true name was not Peter but Pewter or possibly Porter.*

.     .     .     .     .     .     .

Now it should have been observed sooner that there is an obvious division of historical novels into those that present a picture of historical times without special reference to the great people—Kings, Statesmen, etc. —or only incidental mention of them, or an incidental appearance on their part. Other novels present a great person, that is, a historic celebrity and his surroundings. Sir Walter Scott features the Young Pretender in *Waverley,* Richard Coeur de Lion in the *Talisman* and Louis the Eleventh in *Quentin Durward.* But even in these books the times count for more than the men, and in the bulk of Scott's work the main aim is the presentation of bygone days. There is no doubt that this has been the more successful type of historical novel, especially if the times are not too far away and in a place where they speak English or something like it. Conan Doyle's *Micah Clark,* of the days of Monmouth's rebellion, is a fine example. The language is still within reach, the scene (at the time of writing, fifty years ago) still there. So too with the best of the novels and tales of colonial America, as notably, of course, the work of Nathaniel Hawthorne. A good deal of harm was at first done in these American stories by following Walter Scott's lead and putting in the Lady Rowena reappearing in the form of a forest heroine, still talking as volubly as she did with De Bracy in 1189. Indeed she talked even better since the field was more open. The Indians of the Cooper story only "grunted," or occasionally saved up a ration of talk for an Indian harangue. The military men were (fairly) curt in their speech. The heroine got the floor —under the pine trees.

.    .    .    .    .    .    .

But mainly the novel of the not too bygone days has been a success. Not so, in my opinion, the other type, the great people story, and least of all in our immediate times. Leaving out honorable exceptions and not attempting to stigmatize individual names, the newer methods adopted seem pretty tawdry. Thus in order to make a historical character seem real one or two things that he actually did say (according to history) are stuck into his mouth to produce a vivid effect of proved reality. The result is seen in little bits of dialogue patterned like this:

"Good morning, Cardinal," said the housekeeper. "I've brought you your breakfast—two boiled eggs with bacon on the side. That's right, isn't it?"

"Quite right, Jane," said Cardinal Wolsey wearily, rising up on his cushions. "And if I had served my God, Jane, with half the diligence I served my King, he would not have given me over in my grey hairs."

At which the reader reflects with a start, Wolsey *did* say that; I remember it was in the history books. With this method is employed also the introduction of up-to-date language instead of archaic language, as already discussed, a feature that we have to pardon since neither up-to-date nor archaic language seems able to convey the reality, once the language is beyond reach.

A third method, poor stuff in the long run, contrary to true art and permanent value, is the introduction of tit-bits of cruelty and dirt as bait for the reader's attention. It has become only too clear that a sadistic streak has been forming across the pages of our literature, descriptions of cruelty, of torture—that "sell" the book. We can see now that in the past the Victorians loved tears for tears' sake. "I thank you for these tears," wrote the sobbing Lord Jeffrey to Charles Dickens, gulping over the death of little Paul in *Dombey and Son*. The Victorians loved to read of little match girls—meaning little girls who sold matches—going round barefoot in the snow; of little chimney sweeps, selected for their very littleness, stuck in tall chimneys full of soot. Sentiment, as we have seen, was everything in their literature. But at least it seems better than our new greed for scenes of cruelty —next door to cruelty itself.

Still worse is the new dirt, the patches of nasty references, in description or quoted speech, worked into these new historical stories. The best advice to young writers is keep away from it. If you have literary talent and industry you will succeed without it: but if you have once sullied your hand with it, all the sweetmeats of Araby (ask Lady Macbeth) will not clean it. This new dirt cannot be defended as realism, as truth. There is lots of truth that is better left unsaid. Most of it is just put in for the cheapest, the most meretricious of reasons. I do not know whether anyone has actually written a book about Peter the Hermit. But if anyone does it will certainly be like what I have described above. "This book," one reader tells another, "shows that Peter was anything but a hermit: in fact while he was in Syria he contracted . . ." "You don't say!" says the listener. "I must read it."

It is appalling the number of things *contracted* by great people in recent fiction. Poor Napoleon, it seems, contracted everything from barber's itch and hay fever to water on the brain. He died just in time to escape the consequences. In fact as a last advice to young writers of historical fiction I would say, Don't write about Napoleon. It isn't fair. He's had enough.

# CHAPTER IX

## HOW NOT TO WRITE POETRY

*Poets born not made, or born and never made —*
*Poetry antedates prose — Our earliest speech —*
*Splashes and bangs, grunts and gestures — Still belong*
*to infants and apes — Lecture on Gibbon reported by*
*a gibbon ape — Poetry the parent of literature*

EVERYONE knows what poetry is; yet few people would attempt to define it. It reminds us of the quaint old Roman saying, "I know it if you don't ask me." It is easier to say what poetry is not. A piece of writing is not poetry just because it rhymes. Nor is it poetry just because it doesn't rhyme. Nor again does a thing become poetical because it makes no sense as prose and is quite unintelligible to ordinary common sense. Nor will any amount of disturbance of the ordinary rules of grammar, the freedom called "poetic license," in and of itself make poetry, any more than a liquor license can make liquor. In other words both the old idea of rhymed verse turned out to measure and the new idea of free verse turned out to grass are equally erroneous.

In the same way it is difficult, if not impossible, to tell anyone how to write poetry. The old maxim that a poet is born and not made has that much truth in it, though perhaps it ought to read, a poet is born first and then made. The existence of the born poet, and the need of doing something for him to turn him into a made poet is shown by a kind of poetry, or rather of verse, well-known in the pages of rural newspapers and in the rhymed epitaphs of rustic churchyards and affording a standing source of amusement to superior minds. Much of this has been collected into anthologies, gardens as it were of wild flowers. Some writers of this sort of verse have even attained to something like celebrity for the odd mixture of success and failure embodied in it, inspiration without power of expression, high voltage but poor transmission. One thinks of Mrs. Julia Moore, once famous as the "sweet singer of Michigan." Among the treasures of her verse is an *Ode on Lord Byron*—which says:

> *The Character of Lord Byron*
> *Was of a low degree*
> *Caused by his reckless conduct*
> *And bad company—*          and so forth.

Here belongs the Canadian poet McIntyre of Ingersoll, Ontario, the bard of eighty years ago when Ontario first learned the art of cheese-making. He writes:

> *Who hath prophetic vision sees*
> *In future times a ten-ton cheese.*
> *Several companies could join (—or "jine")*
> *To furnish curds for a great combine.*

Yet such writers no doubt are real poets as far as birth can make them so. They lack only the training. Tennyson, born a poet and trained as such, "looked into the future far as human eye could see." So did McIntyre. Tennyson saw a vision:

*Then I dipped into the future far as human eye could*
*        see;*
*Saw the vision of the world, and all the wonder that*
*        would be.——*

McIntyre saw a ten-ton cheese. It's the same thing.

I should wish to make it quite clear that this chapter is not written in depreciation of poetry but only of bad poetry. It is true that the larger part of poetry is bad but the part that is good carries it, and all the best poetry, in its own province and purpose, attains a higher reach than prose. It can call forth, and convey, emotions more poignant and images more vivid than lie within the general reach of prose. It does this by the magic and mystery of words, in part by their melody, in part by leaving aside logical arrangement and consecutive sense.

Tennyson writes:

*Tears, idle tears, I know not what they mean,*
*Tears from the depth of some divine despair*
*Rise in the heart, and gather to the eyes,*
*In looking on the happy autumn fields,*
*And thinking of the days that are no more.*

Prose could not express that. It could make all the statements at greater length in a sustained conservative way. "Happy autumn fields"——that is to say, in the autumn fields where the bright colours of the stubble in the sunshine give the sense of the happiness always associated with light and colour . . . "Divine despair"—that is to say . . . a sense of despair that so much beauty must be so fleeting, but yet with a consoling sense that such despair itself is a proof of man's higher nature. In such a way do professors in a poetry class turn poetry into prose, and when it is done the poetry has somehow vanished like a butterfly out of a net.

Let it be added that poetry also, especially in the English language, falls heir to a number of old words and phrases, in part disused in ordinary speech, and carrying with them all that goes with the peculiar charm of the past.

*In the gloaming, oh, my darling!*

Who couldn't *gloam* at that? "In the evening" doesn't express it. "8:45 P.M." is more exact; the railways prefer it.

*In Flanders fields the poppies blow.*

Yet we couldn't say, "Is there much blowing in your garden this year?"

.      .      .      .      .      .      .

Granted, then, that the writing of poetry rests in the first place on an original bent of mind, it none the less demands a suitable training; and it will be found that a large part of such training consists in learning what to avoid; in other words how not to write poetry. Nor need any literary aspirant claim that he is indifferent to the matter since he has no intention whatever of writing poetry. He can't help himself. Everyone recalls the famous Monsieur Jourdain of Molière's comedy who discovered with surprise that he had been "talking prose" all his life. So every writer of fiction, of history, of anything short of a mathematical text book will realize that part of the time he is writing poetry. If not his writing must be very poor indeed.

. . . . . . .

With which understanding one may with all propriety open a discourse on poetry in order to show that poetry is older than prose, has a higher reach than prose, or rather less range with higher reach, and blends and mingles with prose at its highest.

. . . . . . .

Now by poetry is meant a form of language in which sound and rhythm help to a large degree to carry the sense. Thus, when Swinburne wants to convey to us the aspect and impression of a forsaken garden beside the sea, he writes:

*Over the meadows that blossom and wither,*
*Rings but the note of the sea-bird's song,*
*Only the sun and the rain come hither, all the year*
    *long.*

With that the deserted garden by the sea rises before the eye and the wind sings its desolation. The very sound of the syllables echoes the song of the birds . . . The long-drawn ending *"all the year long"* carries in it the weariness of empty time.

. . . . . . .

Compare again the scenic effect of the opening lines of Gray's famous *Elegy: The lowing herd winds slowly over the lea*—and at the very sound of it we see, or half see in the dusk, the long winding line of cows returning from the pasture. When Gray adds: *And drowsy tinklings lull the distant folds*—he practically has us fast asleep. I remember a college extension lecturer once telling me that at the close of an hour's talk, called *Five Centuries of English Poetry,* he recited Gray's *Elegy* and found, as a curious psychological fact (he said), that a large part of the audience was asleep.

.    .    .    .    .    .    .

Nor is it only the dreariness of deserted gardens and the drowsiness of tinkling folds that the rhythm of words can convey. Take this as putting over the music and the merriment of an Irish party, fiddles, jig and all:

> *Then there was whiskey, and wine for the ladies,*
> *Praties and cakes and bacon and tay,*
> *The Nolans, the Dolans and all the O'Gradys*
> *Were kissing the girls and dancing away.*

It's music before you've even heard the music. Or turn, if you would, to the mournful effect, sorrow sedate and retrained, of such stanzas as the well-known dirge:

> *Here's to the name of poor Tom Bo-owling,*
> *The darling of the crew.*

It may be said that it is only because we know the music that has been set to these words that they convey the effect. But that is not so; the music adds to it; but the effect of the chosen sound, the instinctive harmony, is there before the composer begins. Some songs, grave or gay, wrote themselves into music. The merry verses

of W. S. Gilbert jingle on the page. Kipling's ballads
sing for themselves.

.    .    .    .    .    .    .

*For I'm called Little Buttercup—dear Little Buttercup,*
  *Though I could never tell why,*
*But still I'm called Buttercup—poor Little Buttercup,*
  *Sweet Little Buttercup, I!*

.    .    .    .    .    .

   *My object all sublime*
   *I shall achieve in time—*
 *To let the punishment fit the crime—*
   *The punishment fit the crime;*
   *And make each prisoner pent*
   *Unwillingly represent*
 *A source of innocent merriment!*
   *Of innocent merriment!*

.    .    .    .    .    .

*By the old Moulmein Pagoda, lookin' eastward to the*
   *sea,*
*There's a Burma girl a-settin', an' I know she thinks o'*
   *me;*
*For the wind is in the palm-trees, an' the temple-bells*
   *they say:*
*"Come you back, you British soldier; come you back to*
   *Mandalay!"*

  *Come you back to Mandalay,*
  *Where the old Flotilla lay:*
  *Can't you 'ear their paddles chunkin' from Rangoon*
     *to Mandalay?*
  *On the road to Mandalay,*
  *Where the flyin'-fishes play,*

> *An' the dawn comes up like thunder outer China*
>     *'crost the Bay!*

Now prose—prose that is completely divorced from poetry—cannot obtain these effects. Euclid writes:

*Things that are equal to the same thing are equal to*
    *one another.*

The sound has no connection with the sense except by pure convention, a connection that grew up long after poetry was well on its way. Nor is there any way of matching sense and sound. It is as silent as empty space. There is nothing added if we force it into rhyme:

> *Things that are equal to the same,*
> *Equal to one another we may name.*

Much of the so-called poetry of the Victorian age was made up in just this needless way. Let us try another: *The assessed value of the real estate in the township of Oro has increased by fifty per cent in fifty years.* That's prose and should remain so. A Victorian poet would no sooner read it than he would begin to boil over with something such as:

> *Hail! Oro, township of the Blest*
> *Where real estate is heavily assessed.*

but he doesn't add anything to the first statement.

.     .     .     .     .     .     .

Now if poetry means the use of sounds that of themselves convey meaning, it appears that many of our words are themselves poetry. Such words as *murmur*

nd *babble* and *whisper; rattle* and *roar* and *hiss;
ing-song, lullaby* . . . there are thousands of them.
We can still make them up at will. We make up new
ones, and preserve old ones when we talk to children;
. prose *dog* becomes a poetical *bow-wow.* These poeti-
al words are called in the grammar books onomato-
poetic which is merely and exactly the Greek for poeti-
al words. The grammar books explain that they show
he origin of speech itself and this is partly so, but
only partly. Modern study of the origins of human
peech leads us to observe the parallel primitive forms
used by animals and by ourselves in communicating
with animals and in talking to children. And here we
begin to detect *tones* and *accents* as the major part of
communication, not words at all. We still use these.
We complain in a whine; we threaten in a growl; we
hank with a giggle. We talk to babies in a *yum-yum,
itti-itti* fashion which oddly enough the baby seems to
understand. The baby having just arrived from the
lim cloud land, with the buried memories of life long,
ong ago, understands sounds that for us have been
mothered out by convention. Silly people wish to
avoid baby talk in the nursery. They think that the
baby will learn to speak more quickly without it. This
s exactly the reverse of truth. The baby must get the
ones first, the words (nearly all of them) are just
convention. It is, therefore, proper to say *Did-ums
wantums ikki bit of suggy?* . . . instead of *Would
you care to have a piece of sugar?*

Euclid would have found it hard to explain to his
babies in his nursery—which was probably a rec-
angular tetrahedron with homologous angles—that

"things that are equal to the same thing are equal to
one another." Probably he didn't try; he came into
his nursery and held up one thumb, and said *Boo!* And
then another thumb, just like it, and said *Boo!* And
little Euclids broke out into chuckles, and walked past
axiom one, via poetry.

.        .        .        .        .        .        .

There were not only imitation words (*splash* and
*bang* words) in the dawn of speech, and tones and
growls, but also, so it is claimed, a set of exclamations,
of whoops and puffs, sounds like those a fat man
makes on a hot day; exclamations like the *Yo! Ho!* of
sailors all heaving together. Another primitive origin
is the queer intake of breath in place of the usual out-
put of breath. Most of our talk is made *out* of our
mouth. But we can, and do, revert to a primitive
variant by taking our breath in—swallowing our words
as it were. For proof of this just imagine that you've
heard of a piece of news which excites your disapproval
but doesn't really distress you, such as that Brown has
run off with Jones's wife for the second time, and you
will probably put your tongue against the roof of your
mouth and say *tut-tut* or *chuk chuk* with an intake of
breath. No one taught you this; you got it fifty thousand years ago. Go to Zulu land and you will hear the
"clicks" of Zulu speech, of the Bantu language, that
have preserved and extended it.

So then we have *splashes* and *bangs* and *whoops* and
*yo ho's,* and *tut-tuts* and along with all that a series of
gestures. We wink our amusement, we wave our goodbye, we shrug our shoulders with disapproval and
"beat our breasts"—at least in race memory—over our

sorrow. All of this is preserved in poetry and in the rendering of it. All of this is still seen, in close parallel and resembling it, by anthropologists who study the greater apes. A poet on a platform reciting his verses, with suitable growls and making passes in his hair, is behaving like an ape. They would recognize and welcome him on the Congo.

. . . . . . .

Now anthropologists tell us indeed that many aspects of our speech are parallel to the mode of communication, of the talk, if we can call it so, of the "primates"—a term which in this sense includes the chimpanzee, the gorilla, the orang-outan, etc., but not, of course, the "primates" of the church—archbishops and bishops. The great apes use vocal sounds. The gibbon ape seems to use a set of sound patterns which evoke corresponding answers, but with vocal sounds go also gestures and body movements. When we listen to a hard-luck story and keep saying, Dear me! Dear me! in a hollow voice we are talking like a gibbon ape. Our quick responsive winks and smiles recall the wild chimpanzees who appear to have a crude system of communication by gestures and contacts. When the people (in the Old Testament) expressed their sorrow by beating their breasts they were a poor second to the gorilla whose chest thumping, it has been said, might qualify him for a position as sound producer in a radio broadcasting station.

We can no longer communicate with the apes by direct language, nor can we understand, without special study, their modes of communication which we have long since replaced by more elaborate forms. But it is at least presumable that they could still detect in our speech, at least when it is public and elaborate, the underlying tone values with which it began. Thus if we could take a gibbon ape to a college public lecture, he would not indeed understand it, but he would "get a good deal of it." This is all the students get anyway.

## COLLEGE PUBLIC LECTURE ON EDWARD GIBBON

### AS REPORTED BY A GIBBON APE

The chairman called the audience together with a couple of short barks after which he gave a series of whines to express his disapproval of the lateness of the audience in coming in. He then introduced the lecturer by rubbing his hands together as a sign of pleasure, giving a series of not unfriendly growls in his direction. The lecturer then stood up and rubbed his hands together towards the audience as a sign of good will, opened his lecture with a couple of short yelps which elicited corresponding yelps from the audience. After that he settled down for half an hour to a steady series of grunts which seemed to soothe the listeners. But after this first period the lecturer began to bark, to move up and down, but not threateningly, on the platform, while at times he gurgled in such a friendly manner that a great number of the audience gurgled with him. At times also he heightened the effect of the gurgle by an appealing whine, and closed the lecture with a prolonged howl followed by a final heavy bark. The audience broke into loud yelps and clapped their hands. The chairman then invited another man to give a few satisfied grunts as an expression of thanks—and the meeting broke up, all barking.

．　．　．　．　．　．　．

From all of which we begin to see that poetry is older than prose. Literature begins with poetry. Primitive mankind began its words and music together with singing poetry. The two at first are one, the human voice the only medium, the words the only sound. Then someone invents, or rather uncounted generations slowly contrive, mechanical means of music copied from nature, from the wind whistling in the trees, the waves pounding on the shore. Hence arise wooden drums, clashing cymbals and whistling pipes. Music and words part company, or rather they change to being associates only. Later the breach widens when mankind learns the art of writing. It becomes a very gulf when the mechanics of printing spread the written word. Thus gradually songs changed to books. Literature, as it were, grew prosier and prosier. But poetry remained the senior partner. In classical Greek literature poetry, including the poetic drama, outweighs all the rest. With it appears history, grown from a record of kings' names on a rock to a record of great events and a talk about them. The change is from the singing history of Homer, older than writing, to the written history of Thucydides which even Thucydides couldn't sing. Before the art of writing history had to be sung, in rhythmical words, to the beating of feet or else one couldn't remember it. History thus became the business of "bards." Compare—since there is always a comparison to be made between the evolution of the

race and the evolution of the individual—the rhyming
and singing verses that used to be used to help children to be interested in and to remember history.

*This is William the Conqueror known full well*
*By his Doomsday Book and his curfew bell—*

*—and so on, and on.*

The child of today with his motion pictures and
superb illustrations has got past all that. Rhyme won't
help him for his ideas go past at four to the second,
and he forgets them even faster. To interest him, history must be made coloured or comic.

.        .        .        .        .        .        .

But turning back again to ancient times, we find in
Roman literature the proportion of poetry and prose
turned the other way. Writing was so wide-spread that
the bards passed out and their singing history was
forgotten. Macaulay's *Lays of Ancient Rome* is an
attempt to show what they must have been like if they
were better than they were, and written in good English. The reconstruction was like that of the bones in
Calaveras county, in Bret Harte's society on the Stanislaus, referred to above:

*Then Brown he read a paper and he reconstructed*
*       there,*
*From those same bones an animal that was extremely*
*       rare.*

But Virgil wrote, he didn't sing, his story of Aeneas
in poetry, for by this time a plain and simple meter
had been devised—called technically iambic hexameter
—as a sort of "business suit" for literature. Indeed

the Greeks had used it as far back as the Homeric bards. But it was only good for long, slow stuff that had to be remembered. For real song-talk all sorts of broken, attractive rhythms were used. Again we note that this is the same as with the children today. How instinctively they like the sound of

*Sing a song o' sixpence, a pocketful of rye . . .*

Take that over to the nearest philologian for a laboratory analysis and he'll tell you that that's a Saturnian meter. Try him also with *Jack and Jill went up the hill,* and *Ride a cock-horse to Banbury Cross—* and you have shoved him back to 500 A.D.

But Virgil's readers didn't propose to sing as vigorously as that. They exchanged singing for sing-song, or, if you will, singing turned to what schoolmasters call "scansion." It's queer to think of Mr. Chips, the schoolmaster, two thousand years later, still "scanning" out to his junior boys—

*Arma vir—umque can—o tro—jae qui—primus ab—
    o ris.*

To avoid any accusation of pedantry in quoting Latin let me say that this is the first line of the first book of Virgil and there are people all over the world who know it—and nothing else in the way of Latin. They don't need to. You can go round the world on that, recognized as a man of culture. But I was only saying that Mr. Chips is all that is left of the ancient Roman bard whose job had vanished after he had rocked Rome's cradle. With the Romans, prose soon outweighed poetry. There appeared the histories of

Tacitus and Livy, voluminous and ominous, and presently treatises on law that tipped the scale to the beam.

After the fall of Rome and the wreck of Europe the people in the dark of the Dark Ages couldn't read. So the bards came back to the devastated Roman provinces, as the nightingales come with the darkness. Hence the troubadours and the jongleurs, who sang history as poetry, back at the old trade, fifteen centuries out of date. They straggled on down the centuries, turning up as Welsh bards and Scottish minstrels, till Walter Scott sang the lay of the last one, whose harp, his sole remaining joy, was carried, as we remember from our school days, by an awful boy.

## CHAPTER X

## HOW NOT TO WRITE MORE POETRY

*Victorian days — Verse on everything — Lines to D. F. on the present of a walking stick — Heavy going by the Light Brigade — Mr. Wordsworth and a dog and a skeleton — Case hushed up — Sweet Highland Girl — Oh! Boy! — Miss Eliza Cook and monkey work with the red man's daughter — Verse of today — To a daffodil, remarking its six-lobe corolla — To a house fly as a member of the Diptera — Poets and affectation — Buffeting the wind*

THUS came the poet down the centuries. But he failed to adjust himself to the march of time. He didn't understand what writing and printing had done to him. He went on writing down in poetry—that is, in rhyme and rhythm, in feet and meter—all sorts of long-winded stuff that belonged elsewhere. Each advance in printing and book making and each new wave of expanding education opened the opportunity wider and wider. It is amazing to think of the enormous quantity of narrative verse (long stories in poetry), occasional verse (meaning an event put into rhyme), that appeared in the eighteenth and early nineteenth centuries. The original "source" of poetry, the "spring" from which it sprang, became a rill, the rill a river, and the river a vast lake, part of it bright with waves that sparkled in the sunshine but a lot of it just water over mud flats.

This wave of misplaced poetry reached its widest spread about a hundred years ago. Slowly the art of story-telling and the ability to read drained away its water . . . and finally, not slowly but very rapidly, the moving picture and the radio completely drained the mud flats like a bath with the plug out.

. . . . . . .

In other words it was the Victorian tradition, both in Great Britain and in America, that poetry could be written, indeed had to be written, about everything. If Queen Victoria had another child the Poet Laureate was expected to do something handsome on it. There were verses on the opening of a railway, on the construction of a barge canal, on opening the Crystal Palace and on closing it. With these went the "occasional" poems addressed to single individuals.

*To the lady Fleming, on seeing the Foundation preparing for the erection of Rydal College—To the Infant M.— M.—, Lines to D. F. on receipt of the present of a walking stick—Stanzas to Mr. Q. on his entering Harvard College—Invocation to Harvard College on its receipt of Mr. Q.*

Some of the above examples are actual and some imaginary but no one could distinguish them.

With these personal verses went abstract ones addressed to Happiness, Loveliness, Emptiness, to Solitude, Beatitude and any other abstraction.

Especially did it become a tradition, a fixed idea, that if something striking happened, some incident of courage, danger, horror or some curiosity or coincidence, the Victorian poet must needs write it up. This was all very well for great events—the loss of the *Royal George*, the sinking of the *Birkenhead* and the *Charge of the Light Brigade* at Balaklava. Even then, by good rights, the power of the verse ought to match the majesty of the occasion. Whether it does so or not, each of us must judge for himself but to my mind many of our treasured poems depend as treasures on our pride in the event. Judged simply as poetry, what are we to think of *Half a league, half a league . . .* and all the blue-water verse, *Ho! mariners of England . . . Ho! Tars . . . Ho! England!*—verses only preserved by the salt wind of the sea and glorious with the recollection of victory.

Still more is this the case with the hymns of the church, whose long echoes and cadences go back through generations and some through centuries, of human joy and sorrow, of sabbath worship and evening song. Some people may recall the outbreak of popular anger—it must be forty years ago—over the statement of a Chicago Professor of English that many of the hymns of the churches are doggerel. He was undoubtedly right. Devout people without logic wrote to the newspapers to ask—what about *Lead kindly light?*—what about *Nearer my God to Thee?*—and the majestic words and music of *Come, all ye faithful, joyful and triumphant*—a chant that reverberates from the days of the Christians in Rome. Such argument, of course, has nothing to do with the case. Some of the hymns, many of the hymns—can we say the majority of the hymns?—are certainly doggerel. They are saved only by the spirituality of the background. Taken as poetry, as language, they are filled with crude phrases, and especially with those mixed up metaphors which seem, as we have said, the especial privilege of the church and of clergymen. The clergy, as is natural to their calling, look to the reality of meaning and ignore the mere form of words.

We are thus willing to accept and condone the tribute applied in the past to great natural events, or written into hymns now sanctified by time. All of this because it is part of our heritage. But it does not follow that we need try still to appreciate narratives of minor bygone events done into verse after the fashion of the period, still less to imitate them now.

We take an example from Wordsworth.

Wordsworth hears of a pathetic incident, happening on his rugged Cumberland, concerning the fidelity of a dog. The dog's master had fallen over a cliff and the faithful animal had watched beside his master's body for several months, before the body was found— a skeleton. The incident is indeed striking and pathetic, and, of course, depends for its pathos on its truth. If it were a made-up story we could get little "kick" out of it unless we said that the dog stayed for two years, or that there were several dogs, the first one and then friends who joined him, working in relays. But although the story is true it does not follow that the best way to convey its truth is to put it into rhyming verses. To me, the rhyming form lends it something false, something unnatural.

The poem begins:

*A barking sound the shepherd hears,*
*A cry as of a dog or fox,*
*He halts and searches with his eye*
*Among the scattered rocks—*

There seems something so pit-pat, dead certain, about the fall of the syllables that they hide the reality under the adornment.

*And presently a dog is seen*
*Glancing through that covert green.*

Naturally then the shepherd becomes curious and proceeds to look round to account for the dog's actions.

But the poet refuses to disclose what happens till he gets the full scene set.

*It was a cove, a huge recess,*
*That keeps, till June, December's snow;*
*A lofty precipice in front,*
*A silent tarn below!*

*Thither the rainbow comes—the cloud—*
*And mists that spread the flying shroud;*
*And sunbeams; and the sounding blast,*
*That, if it could, would hurry past;*
*But that enormous barrier holds it fast.*

Now, then be ready for the shepherd. Aha! he's struck something:

*Nor far has gone before he found*
*A human skeleton on the ground.*
*The appalled discoverer with a sigh*
*Looks round to learn its history . . .*

A "sigh" for a skeleton is mild enough. It reminds us of our mention of *Punch's* detective, Hector Trumper, who gazed at the spectacle of the mangled body and accustomed as he was to scenes of violence, could hardly "suppress a yawn." Not only is the sigh a short one but it is followed by a hurried explanation that the spectator now instantly

> . . . *Recalls the name*
> *And who he was and whence he came;*
> *Remembers, too, the very day*
> *On which the stranger passed that way.*

All this in a hurry because the poet has used too much time on the poetic description of the scene of the tragedy. This is not to be a crime mystery. So the shepherd also instantly recalls "who he was and whence he came," etc., etc. So that everything of that sort can be left to the police at the inquest.

Very naturally, the stranger had fallen over the cliff and had been killed. His body lay there till it became a wasted skeleton. The poem ends with an allusion to the dog, typical of the piety that was part of the poetry of the period:

> *How nourished there through that long time*
> *He knows who gave that love sublime*
> *And gave that sense of feeling great*
> *Beyond all human estimate.*

Such was the method of narrative poetry, in its relation to minor incidents of a hundred years ago. I do not think there is room for such poetry now. There may, or may not, be room for vast epic narratives in verse of the history of the United States and such exalted topics. But for the minor stuff there is no place, except as comic poetry, intentional or accidental. Other methods of presentation—the radio, the moving picture—have replaced it. Indeed such events now naturally come to us as newspaper items. Here is Wordsworth's Dog Story as it would read in the report of the inquest held on the unfortunate stranger. We take it from the files of the *Cumberland Weekly Shepherd*:

### Fidelity of a Canine

*Mr. W. Wordsworth in his evidence at the inquest arising from the recent Dog and Cliff Mystery gave his account of the gruesome discovery of a human skeleton at the base of Skaw Cliff. Mr. Wordsworth was led to the discovery by the strange behaviour of a dog which was darting in and out of the bracken at the foot of the cliff as if to attract attention. Investigation revealed the dead body of a man, reduced by exposure to little more than a skeleton, having evidently laid there for over two months.*

*Indeed Mr. Wordsworth himself remembers having met a stranger, now to be identified only by his clothes, walking with a dog along the dangerous brow of the cliff. He recalls indeed having uttered a warning to the effect that the place where the stranger was standing was really a cove, a huge recess, with a silent tarn below. Mr. Wordsworth says that he explained to the stranger the peculiar meteorological aspect of the spot, a gathering place for rainbows, and cloud and mist, with occasional sunshine and the sounding blast that endeavoured in vain to hurry past, but was held fast, as Mr. Wordsworth explained, by the enormous barrier itself. Mr. Wordsworth was pained to notice that the stranger had moved off while he was still making his explanation, and that the attempt to follow him and repeat it was prevented by the ominous growling of the dog. He thought no more of the incident until his finding of the body, the man having apparently fallen, or plunged, over the cliff immediately after the conversation. Mr. W. is unable to account for the dog having found nourishment during his long vigil. "God knows how that dog got food," he said.*

.    .    .    .    .    .    .

So much for the tediousness of the bygone poetic narrative. Equally typical of the period is the overdone sentiment that runs to feeble sentimentality. Every epoch has the defects of its qualities. The days of Tennyson and Longfellow, of Hawthorne and Dickens were days of increasing "humanitarianism," the new sympathy with the oppressed and with the lowly and the new appreciation of the still beauty of lowly natural scenery, the dell secluded from the ruder world. But there was no need to get mawkish about it, and to allow sympathy to degenerate into drivel. An excellent example is found again in Wordsworth's work, this time in his well-known poem addressed to a *Highland Girl*. The theme of the poem is that the poet comes suddenly upon a Highland girl among the beautiful scenery of a Highland glen. He proceeds, after the fashion of poets of the time, to do what was called "apostrophize her." "Sweet Highland girl," he exclaims:

> . . . *a very shower*
> *Of beauty is thy earthly dower!*
> *Twice seven consenting years have shed*
> *Their utmost bounty on thy head*
> *And these grey rocks; that household lawn;*
> *Those trees, a veil just half withdrawn;*
> *This fall of water that doth make*
> *A murmur near the silent lake;*
> *This little bay; a quiet road*
> *That holds in shelter thy abode—*
> *In truth together do ye seem*
> *Like something fashioned in a dream.*

This is all very well and very charming, but the poet doesn't let it go at that. He is carried on still further to the idea that he would like to come and live alongside of the girl:

> *Oh happy pleasure (he cries), here to dwell*
> *Beside thee in some healthy dell,*
> *Adopt your homely ways and dress,*
> *A shepherd! thou a shepherdess!*

To get the full kick out of this, one would have to add the American exclamation, "Wow!" One can imagine the poet changing into his Highland costume behind a bush and calling out—"Now, don't look! Wait a minute!"

Nor is that enough. He feels that even with a kilt on he'd like to get nearer still, into some sort of family contact with the girl.

> *What joy to hear thee, and to see!*
> *Thy elder brother I would be!*

*Thy father—anything to thee!* (Here he ought to add
    "Oh, Boy!")

I remember that when I was a master at school a
pupil in the reading-aloud class brought to the poem
an even higher pitch of sentiment, quite unconsciously,
by reading it slowly and doggedly out, word by word.

*What-joy-to-hear-thee-and-to-see-thy-elder-brother!*

This beat even Wordsworth who failed to get anything as flat and final as that. Indeed the poet could
find no other dénouement except what he said at the
start:

> *Thee, neither know I, nor thy peers;*
> *And yet my eyes are filled with tears.*

In other words,—sit down and let's have a good cry.

.    .    .    .    .    .    .

Another form of false sentiment of the period was
to create purely imaginary wrongs suffered by purely
imaginary people . . . England—the mind of the
people—was determined that all tyranny must end, all
oppressed people be given freedom. The idea was
mixed with other things, Manchester cotton, Sheffield
cutlery, etc., but in the main it was a noble aspiration.
It meant, however, that the poets must work overtime to find oppressed people, patriotic Greeks, noble
Italians, etc. But these kept getting disqualified by diplomatic changes in British policy which shifted them
to the wrong side. So a regular stand-by was found in
the Red Indian. Ever since Alexander Pope had written his, *Lo, the Poor Indian,* the Red Man, understood

to be vanishing, to be moving to the sunset, drew the tears of the English nursery, and kindled the indignation of the English heart and hearth.

.    .    .    .    .    .    .

This particular kind of tripe reaches its acme, or one of its acmes, in a poem by Eliza Cook called the *Song of the Red Man*. I wish that a Pottawattomie "brave" or a Seneca cannibal could have read it. Miss Eliza Cook flourished (1818-89), and flourished exceedingly. Her collected works, at forty lines to the page and two and one-half inches to the line, represent a mile of poetry. It is all forgotten now except the verses in which she asks who shall dare to chide her for loving an old armchair—a challenge which got into the American school books and was never taken up. She had no further knowledge of Red Indians than what can be learned at Wimbledon. But she saw that a Red Indian was good medicine. Her Red Indian—exact location not specified—lives quietly in his "maize-covered grounds" under a "date-shadowed roof." Presumably the dates are 1492 and that of the Louisiana Purchase, 1803, things that must have shadowed Indian life. He lives, as he says himself, content—simple fellow—with his "rifle and hounds." He had saved and befriended a wandering white man, and now it appears the white man is starting what has been called since Miss Cook's time, "monkey work" with the Indian's daughter. In fact he says,

*I saw you last night where the linden trees grow*
*With my child in the leafy savanna below.*

The location is again puzzling, but the danger is obvious. He, therefore, suggests,

*Go! leave me, false man, while my child is secure.*

. . . and in order to establish the reasonableness of this proposition, he adds,

*Should a lily-skinned daughter e'er cling to thy neck,*
*Then remember the father whose peace thou would'st*
*    wreck.*

*Lily-skinned* is good but perhaps *onion-skinned* is even daintier.

. . . . . . .

But let us turn from pulling the mote out of the Victorian eye to removing the beam from our own. The poet is indeed incorrigible. Time and circumstance no sooner remove one set of faults than he develops new ones in a contrary direction. He is no sooner cured of the artificial regularity of rhymed verse than he degenerates in the pointless irregularity of verse that is called "free." He is no sooner taught to avoid long, prosy narrative poetry, than he substitutes short, prosy descriptive poetry. We no sooner persuade him to stop crying and not be sentimental than he gets dirty and objectionable.

. . . . . . .

The form of the verse, or its formlessness, is one thing. Its content another, and the present content of a great deal of our contemporary poetry runs to the description of nature, in minute detail with great exactitude, but with no particular merit in the detail. This nature poetry is the illegitimate child of our new natural science. In natural science detail is admirable. It is excellent to distinguish, as we do, the cephalopods from the infusoria and to classify, as we do, fifty thousand species of flies, and to confer on them a scientific order as the Diptera which makes them sound as old as the Italian nobility. But this is not poetry. It is not possible to make poetry by the mere cumulation of detail, by putting scenery together tree by tree and leaf by leaf. Nor does close observation of nature at work in and of itself make poetry.

It is, as I have dared to suggest above, especially in Canada that this new nature poetry grows at its rankest. The really fine Canadian poets, both of the generation just gone by and of the generation now writing, are too well-known and too well-established to fear criticism of their methods. The fact that most of them owe their success to nature-description-poetry does not make any more tolerable the great mass of the description in verse, whether free or worth money, of the Canadian woods, trees, birds, beasts and waterfalls. Our country is rich in its extent. Granting a thousand poets as the maximum that we could raise they have three thousand square miles for each of them to work on.

Contrast the almost magical effects of description achieved by earlier poets without seeming to describe . . . Compare, for we owe him one, Wordsworth:

> *Oh, then my heart with rapture fills*
> *And dances with the daffodils*

Or Herrick:

> *Fair daffodils we weep to see*
> *You haste away so soon . . .*

With how few words, with how little of the intricacies of description, either poet calls up a picture of the yellow, dancing flowers. Now compare the painful piece-work description as done by an up-to-date poet, and written in free verse, since we could hardly expect rhyme to be thrown in with anything so difficult as that:

*You, O, daffodil! standing on*
  *My table in a glass of water,*
*I recognize you with the help of the Ency-*
      *clopaedia Britannica,*
*As the pseudo-narcissus, a member of the family Ama-*
      *rillaccoe.*
  *Your stem is about 18 in. long.*
  *I note the spathe, single flowered.*
  *I observe your corolla, cleft into six lobes.*
  *I see the central bell-shaped nectary*
              *O, you daffodil*
                  *I'm on!*

As with the life of the flowers and plants, so with the higher life of the birds. How easily the real poet calls them to the sky. We take Shelley, with his skylark, "singing still dost soar, and soaring ever singest." Or, we return a moment to Swinburne's *Forsaken Garden* . . . where "rings but the note of the seabirds' song." Compare with these some of the latest animal life efforts in free verse, mere accuracy of description substituted for the open inspiration of the sky. . . .

## TO A HOUSE FLY

*O, you musca domestica, peeping at me in the morn-*
*ing sun, from the foot of the bed*
*I recognize in you one of the merry boys*
*of the Diptera,*
*I know you by your single pair of*
*membranous wings.*
*Have you an anterior pair? No, only in*
*aberrant exceptions.*
*But I would know you anywhere by your*
*proboscis,*
*And by your haunting eyes, compound eyes,*
*with movable lenses.*
*Don't tell me how you work them, no, please!*
*Don't come nearer,*
*You might give me malaria or elephantiasis,*
*Come one step nearer, and,—*
*Swot! I got you.*

.     .     .     .     .     .     .

One decided step towards writing poetry, to the extent of one's native talent, is to get rid of that certain affectation which surrounds the making of poetry.
Round poetry and the poet clings a sort of atmosphere of superiority over work-a-day occupations and
straightforward activities. But this superiority is only
justified in so far as it holds true for all creative art,
for art for art's sake, as opposed to occupation for
money's sake. Even in this, though the activity is low,
it may be, and mostly is, elevated by a decent motive
such as earning one's daily bread and that of other

people. Moreover the principle of creative art may step in anywhere as a sort of inspiration, the fairyland compensation to those who have to work. Where this happens any craftsman becomes a "poet," in the original sense of one who makes something, whether he is a joiner making a table, or a tailor dreaming, with uplifted scissors, of a new daring in a spring overcoat. Even an honest day's work, something attempted, something done, as with Longfellow's blacksmith, became a sort of art. Thus does necessity impose work on the human race, and imagination slip out of its fetters.

Yet the poet, odd fellow, must have his way, with his velvet coat and his loose tie and his long hair. Loose and easy is his motto. Nothing must impede his breath or choke his chest.

This affectation of the trade has affected not only mock poets but real ones, great ones. Alfred Tennyson, especially as he grew old and turned into Lord Tennyson, displayed just such a pose. He dressed the part. He loved to stride along the sea shore of the Isle of Wight, a cloak thrown carelessly across his shoulder, thus buffeting the wind, or letting the wind buffet him —I forget which. But he needed someone there to see him buffet.

Some readers may recall a distinguished British poet of yesterday, lecturer to American audiences, who used to carry this pose to the platform. He had a way of passing his hand sideways across his forehead before beginning to read his piece and saying, "This *came* to me in the heart of the woods" . . . either there or in a place that he called "the crowded mart." But if a lecturer on economics said that he got his idea on wages in the bush, or down town, it wouldn't make the same kind of hit. Yet the one is just as likely as the other. Anybody can be absorbed anywhere. An engineer can dream of a fly-wheel without calling himself a glow worm.

There is no need, therefore, for a man who wishes to be a poet to adopt the pose of a do-nothing dreamer. It may be those who do most, dream most.

# CHAPTER XI

## HOW TO WRITE HUMOUR

*Telling funny stories — Perhaps you've heard this one!
— Humour and kindliness — The primitive laughter of the gods — Fun with words — Puns — Bad
spelling — Burlesque writing — Cannibalism in the
Cars — A pension for life if dead in five years — Pure
and impure limericks*

VERY few people undertake to write humour, or even
aspire to do so. But a great many people undertake to
tell funny stories which is a branch of the same thing.
A few people tell them well, but if they do, they are
apt to get over-comic and over-conscious. A few tell
them with brevity and humility dictated by modesty.
But most people tell them with a prolixity and an in-
competence which are deplorable. This is all the more
deplorable in as much as in many social circles funny
stories, told in turn, and even out of turn, are part of
the stock-in-trade. At the end of each story silence
falls, everybody trying to think of another. "Nothing
is heard," said Bill Nye, "but the rumble of a thinker."

At the time when Bill Nye flourished there was
more excuse for funny stories as the mainstay of a
dinner or supper party than there is now. There was
very little for everybody to talk about that everybody
else knew about. The moving pictures have changed all

that. Conversation can now be carried on along such familiar lines as:

"Did you see *The Silver Dagger* last week?"

"No, I didn't see it. Did you see *The Golden Bullet* the week before?"

"No, I didn't."

"You should have seen it."

"My sister saw it in Schenectady."

"Did she? My mother saw it in Troy."

That kind of thing is as easy and as endless as exercises in French. If it is not conversation it is at least a good substitute. It can be varied at will by shifting to:

"Did you hear Charlie McCarthy last week?"

"Yes, we always do."

"He's great!"

"He is, isn't he? What was it he said last Sunday— about a cow?"

"About a cow?"

"Yes, about a cow— Jane, what was it Charlie McCarthy said last Sunday about a cow?"

"I don't remember."

"Anyway, it was darned good."

One would think that people with resources such as that available would not fall back on telling one another funny stories. But they do. A few stories are so short, so excellent, so fool-proof in the telling, that they are worth while in any case and they get over. The laughter that greets them is genuine and their repetition assured. But this is only true of the ideal funny story when given at least half a chance.

By a fool-proof story we mean one of such a simple outline, such a plain setting, without details of place, description and character, that there is no need to introduce extraneous matter, indeed little possibility of doing so. Of such nature are the little generalized "tags" about "Scotchmen," "old darkies," "Jews," "commercial travellers" and other such people whose character supposedly is reduced to one word, and who live everywhere, always, thus:

*What is the difference between a Scotchman and a canoe? A canoe tips.*

*An Irish doctor's bill to a lady: For Curing Your Husband Till He Died.*

*Notice on a Jewish golf course: Members Will Please Not Pick Up Lost Balls While Still Rolling.*

Next in rank above these simple little tags come "stories"—events told in two or three sentences, so simple in the sequence of ideas, and turning on some easily remembered phrase, that they practically tell themselves. Thus:

*A London medical professor who had received a royal appointment put a notice up in his classroom:*
*Professor Smith begs to inform his students that he has been appointed physician to the King.*
*A student wrote underneath it:*
*God save the King.*

Anyone can tell that story who will keep a firm grip on the key to it—God save the King.

.    .    .    .    .    .    .    .

Take a similar key-phrase story which went round the civilized world a few years ago tightly bound up to the phrase "a little stiff from Polo." It was usually told by saying that a young man at a dance started an apology by saying, "I'm afraid I can't dance very well; I'm just a little stiff from Polo" . . . and the girl said, "That's all right; I don't care where you come from; let's try it anyhow."

.     .     .     .     .     .     .

Such stories are so simple that they even are apt to carry a sort of appendix tagged to them of how an "Englishman" tried to repeat the story and said: "I'm just a little stiff from cricket" . . . and added later, somewhat puzzled, "I'm not quite sure it was cricket; it may have been something else." . . . An "Englishman" in these cases means a man without humour.

But the moment you get beyond this simple range a funny story demands a few details and permits a lot. Take again the world famous story, "Put me off at Buffalo." Everybody knows how it ends with the porter's rueful exclamation—"Well, if you're not the gentleman I put off at Buffalo, who was?"

But plain as it is, there are people who can spoil even that story by saying that the Wabash through train goes through Buffalo at about 3:30 A.M.—and then saying, "No, not the Wabash—the other one—that line up from—you know—no, not the Lehigh—anyway, it doesn't matter—oh, yes, of course, the Lackawanna. Well, this feller had a lower berth, or say, a berth on the Lackawanna for Chicago due in Buffalo . . . and so on—till the next bump.

.     .     .     .     .     .     .

I recommend to any student of humour, next time he is listening to a funny story, to observe how much extraneous matter it contains which has nothing to do with the point.

Even before the extraneous matter is reached, the story is apt to be damaged by the speaker's interpolation, "Have you heard this?"—followed a little later by—"You haven't heard this?"

Now just as a matter of critical study note some of the commonest ways of damaging or destroying a funny story.

1. Moving backwards instead of forwards—sample:
*My father used to tell a good story about the darkies. Father, you know, was born down in Georgia. He only moved up here later on. In fact he was out west for years and years in between. That was where he met mother. Her old man, I may have told you, was one of the forty-niners . . .* and so on, back to the Louisiana Purchase.

2. Too many narrators; sample:
*I heard a good story from a feller on the train who was telling me about camping out with a feller, and this feller had a great yarn about two fellers. . . .* Six, so far, isn't it? Or is it ten?

3. Many people, and in this case especially genial and easy-going, remember the fun they got out of a story but forget the point. Such a man will begin, with a laugh of appreciation:
*. . . I heard old Doc Noble get off a darned good one the other night. Jim Thompson—you know Jim—*

*always comes dropping into the surgery but he's never sick, just wants to borrow a dollar. But the other night he came in and said, "Doc, I'm a sick man" . . . and the old doctor says—story teller begins to laugh— what the hell was it he said . . . darned good anyway . . .*

4. But more complete havoc can be made by mishandling the point of the story.

Humorous narration, as we shall see in detail later, may be made amusing all through, or lead up to an amusing end without being amusing till it gets there. This laughable ending, this "nub," as it has been called, is all there is in most funny stories as related by ordinary people. Most of them, modestly enough, struggle towards it as fast as they can. They want to *get* to it and have the fun of hearing people laughing at it. . . . But a certain infernal type of story teller holds it off, loves to keep it in suspense to pile up the expectation— regardless of the strained faces and the suffering minds of the listeners.

*Example:* Here is, I imagine, one of the best known stories in the world. It is a story with a nub in it and utterly dependent on the nub without which there is nothing in it. Plainly told, it reads:

*A miserable man, evidently in poor health, came to the consulting office of a Parisian doctor. The doctor examined him pretty thoroughly and then said reassuringly: "Well, my dear sir, there's absolutely nothing wrong with you except overstrain and worry. What you need to do is forget your work, enjoy yourself, have a good laugh. Why not go and see this new come-*

*dian Coquelin that they're all talking about? . . ."*
*"Pardon me," said the patient sadly, "I am Coquelin."*

. . . . . . .

Now, one type of story-killer could spoil this by letting the cat out of the bag at once and beginning:

*It seems that this fellow Coquelin, the great French funny actor, was a pretty miserable specimen to look at. Anyway he went in one day to a doctor's office, etc. etc.*

But the other type of story-teller holds the cat so tight in the bag that it's dead when it gets out.

Thus:

*A fellow came into a French doctor's office one day and looked pretty tough, not exactly ill, but, oh, sort of run down and mean looking, though you couldn't say . . . etc. etc. etc.* (Help!)

*So the doctor looked him all over, and punched him up and down and tried the stethoscope on him, and tapped his chest . . . etc. etc. etc.* (Help!)

*So at last he said, "Well, I tell you, there's nothing really the matter with you, you're run down, of course, and in bad shape and your blood pressure is perhaps a little bit high, but, take it all in all, you're not in any way ill in the real sense. . . .*

What the narrator deserves, and sometimes gets at this point, is that some one should break in, quite innocently,

"Well, that's often the way. I knew a fellow out home that was just like that, always complaining, and yet . . ."

"Well, this fellow . . ."

"Same sort of case, old Doc Rykert said himself . . ."

"No, but I hadn't finished."

"Oh, I'm sorry. Did he die in the office?"

. . . . . . .

As with poetry, everybody knows what humour is
until he tries to define it. The difficulty is all the
greater because we use the word in two senses, sometimes to mean something in ourselves, our "sense of
humour," and at other times to mean the "humour
of a situation," as if it were something outside of ourselves. The fact is it means both, for the two concep-
tions are like the clapper and the bell, the hammer
and the anvil. To put it in the academic language of
philosophy, one term is subjective, the other objective.

It is hard to think of a sense of humour in a vacuum
with nothing to get humorous about. It sounds like being crazy. It is equally hard to think of "funny hap-
penings" in a purely physical sense. Euclid may have
roared with laughter when a perpendicular fell on a
line, but no one else could have. Hence comes our in-
and-out use of language, by which humour means
either a human quality or the outside contacts that
bring it into play.

The best definition of humour that I know is: *Humour may be defined as the kindly contemplation of
the incongruities of life and the artistic expression
thereof.* I think this the best I know because I wrote
it myself. I don't like any others nearly as well. Students of writing will do well to pause at the word
*kindly* and ponder it well. The very essence of humour
is that it must be kindly. "Good jests," said King

Charles the Second, that most humorous and kindly king who saved monarchy in England, "ought to bite like lambs, not dogs; they should cut, not wound." The minute they begin to bite and wound that is not humour. That is satire and as it gets more and more satirical the humour dries out of it, leaving only the snarl and rasp of sarcasm. To quote from a poem from which I am never tired of quoting, Bret Harte's *Society on the Stanislaus.* We remember that when Jones claimed that the fossil bones reconstructed by Brown into a Palaeozoic animal were only one of his lost mules, Brown retorted by apologizing for having trespassed on Jones's family vault.

*He was a most* sarcastic *man, this kind Mr. Brown.*

Here we have it exactly. *Sarcastic,* as intended to rasp Jones's feelings—the derivation of the word is a hoe or rasp. Yet observe that though Mr. Brown is sarcastic the poem itself is humorous. There's nothing unkind in that—seen as it were in a far-away focus.

Hence the more you look at it the more you will see that all truly great humour, all the great humorous characters are portrayed through a medium of kindliness. Falstaff is really a despicable creature; give him all the world and he'd take it, but after all he asks nothing at the moment but a bellyful—a large bellyful—of sack, a pipe of tobacco and somebody to talk at. The humour of him lies in our forgiveness of him. Our higher selves take a broader view. Don Quixote, the Vicar of Wakefield, Rip Van Winkle, Mr. Pickwick—each one is surrounded by an atmosphere of kindliness. Life seems a better thing in their society.

The fundamental basis, then, for writing humour is to share in this human kindliness, to develop to the full extent what native share we have of it, and to look in that direction for our judgment of our fellow men.

Humour probably began with pretty primitive stuff. So did laughter. Most likely it was some kind of triumphal grunt or shout of exultation over victory . . . and humour probably began as a similar sense of triumph in seeing something knocked out of shape, or offering a sort of contradiction of nature—such as a cow with two heads. The Greek gods—their intelligence was very low—thought it funny when Hephaestus (or somebody) fell out of Heaven and broke his leg and walked with a limp. Heaven echoed with the laughter of the gods. It must have been a hell of a heaven.

Human beings, not being gods, found, as they themselves developed, that their sense of enjoyment of this kind of disaster must depend on its being really harmless, the disaster only an appearance. On these terms it is still "funny" to us when a man's hat blows off and he chases it out in the street. To a Greek god it would be funnier still if a bus ran over him.

Here again, as everywhere, children repeat individually the development of the race collectively. Nursery humour is full of slaughter, disaster and sudden death. Welsh giants are fooled by Jack the Giant Killer into ripping their stomachs open. Suitors seeking the Sleeping Beauty die spiked on thorn hedges. People get boiled in pots, chopped in little pieces—all sorts of fun.

You can see this upward progress of humour all through the ages. Here we have the humour of primitive cruelty replaced by the practical jokes of the Middle Ages. This itself was pretty rough stuff. In the castle hall some one is beguiled into—no, some one is fooled into—putting his head outside to see what sort of night it is and some one else drops a turnip on his head from an upper window. The practical joke died hard. It is, indeed, not quite dead. Schoolboys still put bent pins on masters' chairs. But here is not so much humour as retribution.

The simplest attempts at humorous, or call it comic, writing consist of trying to get fun out of words themselves. This includes such things as pun-making, bad spelling, comic dialect, and so on. The humour is supposed to lie in the oddity of the sound and sense, the incongruity of the verbal forms thus created, as differing from the "correct" forms. With this goes in some measure, as with the pun-maker, the attraction of ingenuity. This is the same impulse that leads people into strenuous effort over crossword puzzles. The man in a railway car who murmurs "a river in ancient Greece," "a curved sword in seven letters," is the same man who would have made puns when Queen Victoria was young. . . .

.    .    .    .    .    .    .

Puns on the American side of the Atlantic have lost almost all literary, social and commercial value. People generally greet a pun with a groan. In England the pun refuses to die, or at least to stay dead. A pun means putting two different meanings that belong to the same word or phrase into unexpected juxtaposition. The clash of sound and sense is supposed to excite our sense of humour by its incongruity, a thing similar to the "funny" effect of a clown in a tiny round hat.

Very likely in its origin the pun was perhaps not so much a funny effect as a serious one, a way of calling attention. The famous pun of Pope Gregory on the fair-haired Anglo-Saxon children in the Roman slave market—Gregory's mixture, as some one once called it, when there *was* a Gregory's mixture—this pun, I say, was meant in seriousness, almost in sadness. "These are not Angles," he said, "they're *angels.*" The play upon words was not play, but earnest, as if to say, "What do you know about that?" So, too, I imagine with the famous puns of Shakespeare, like the well known words of John of Gaunt:

> *Old Gaunt indeed and Gaunt in being old.*

But if the pun ever had such an exalted status it lost it entirely in Victorian England when puns became the order of the day as the stock-in-trade of funny men and comic papers. The technique of illustration at that time was quite inadequate for the delightful humorous cartoons of our present press and the merry fun of the comic strips. Hence all burlesque and comic writing relied greatly on puns. Even the Houses of Parliament and the Ministry appreciated a pun. Witness the famous example in 1843 when all official and academic England roared with laughter when Sir Charles Napier ended his message about his conquest of Sind with the Latin word *"Peccavi."* (*I have sinned.*) Later on, but not till everybody was dead, it was disclosed that Napier didn't mean to make a pun at all. He just meant that he admitted having exceeded his authority, and he said it with a familiar schoolboy term, *Peccavi.*

(I'm in the wrong.) British schoolboys then and long after used Latin tags such as *Peccavi!* and *Pax!* etc. Napier himself hadn't noticed the pun. But the story, true or apocryphal, illustrates the period.

Consider the case of Tom Hood (1799-1845). His *Song of the Shirt* published in *Punch*, Christmas, 1843, is one of the memorials of English social history. But Hood had to publish it without his name for fear people might think it funny. For Hood was an incurable pun-maker, pouring forth his puns in the *Comic Journal* that he carried on. *Punch*, of course, at that time just starting life (1841), was not a funny paper. It was in its origins, as its biographer and brilliant contributor, Mr. Charles L. Graves, has said, "a radical and democratic paper, a resolute champion of the poor, the desolate and the oppressed." Its early pages are grim with the pictures of hunger and misery and want. The *Song of the Shirt* was just right for *Punch*, but not its punning author. Later on, as *Punch* grew wiser, being unable to set all the world right, it replaced biting satire with mellow humour and puns blossomed on its pages. Nor have they ever died out. Even the heroic war numbers of the present hour carry their proper ration of puns.

Hood himself tried to claim that puns were a legitimate form of literary expression.

> *However critics may take offense*
> *A double meaning has double sense.*

But this is only true when it is true. A double meaning may leave nothing more than its jangle of sounds without adding anything to the sense.

Take some of Hood's own:

> *Ben Battle was a soldier bold*
> *And used to war's alarms,*
> *But a cannon ball took off his legs*
> *And he laid down his arms.*

There is absolutely nothing in this but words and sounds. Very different is the case where the use of a pun suggests, or seems to suggest, some further meaning, as when a witty householder called his gas bill the *Charge of the Light Brigade*.

Hood lived up to his creed. He died with a pun, if not on his lips, at least on his pen. He had fallen into illness and poverty and Sir Robert Peel, the prime minister, contrived for him a small pension of which he only lived to receive a first instalment. Hood, dying, wrote his thanks. "It is death that stops my pen, you see, not a *pen*sion."

We may quote again the Latin proverb which tells us that we may throw nature out with a fork but it is bound to come back sooner or later. So it is with play upon words. We no sooner expel it in the form of puns than it comes back in a new shape. Thus we get the "nearly-alike" and the "only a little different" pairs of words which make amusing nonsense even to our present day eyes. The little book of burlesque British History, *1066 and All That* (1930), which met such an uproarious success owed much of it to the new verbal forms.

One may quote a few among the hundreds of these wilful confusions of verbal forms: *The Saxons worshipped dreadful Gods of their own called Monday,*

*Tuesday, Wednesday, Thursday, Friday and Satur-
day . . . There came Waves of Danes accompanied
by their sisters, or sagas . . . the Pheasants' Revolt,
to find out which was the gentleman when Adam
delved and Eve span (the answer being, of course,
Adam). Napoleon's armies always marched on their
stomachs, shouting Vive l'Interieur.*

This is marvellous stuff and we can laugh over it
as our grandfathers laughed over puns and bad spelling. As mere method it would in time become as stale
as puns themselves. But a lot of it contains an underlying basis of real significance, on which humour can
still stand when mere method has worn tattered. It
is the difference between a statue and a scarecrow.

Along with British puns there flourished at the
same epoch American bad spelling. This made no hit
in England as over there people mostly couldn't spell.
We recall what was said in the first chapter about the
66 per cent of English brides of that day who signed
their "mark" instead of their names in the marriage
register. But in America the little red schoolhouse
brought spelling everywhere and the "spelling bee"
turned it to diversion. Hence bad spelling was "funny"
as a sort of take-off of good spelling. It was, so to
speak, a laugh on the spelling book. It is so completely
gone now that it makes Artemus Ward and Orpheus
C. Kerr (Office Seeker) tough reading for the present
generation.

It is proper also to distinguish between bad spelling
used for bad spelling's sake and bad spelling when used
to indicate the bad pronunciation of the characters
concerned. Herein lies the difference between Bill Nye

and Josh Billings and Artemus Ward on the one hand
and such writers as James Whitcomb Riley and Eugene Field on the other. Here, for example, is Josh
Billings (Henry Wheeler Shaw, 1818-1884) writing
on *Laughter* and speaking in his own person, not quoting the talk of a character:

*In konclusion i say laff every good chance yu kan
git, but don't laff unless yu feal like it, for there ain't
nothing in this world more harty than a good honest
laff. . . . When you do laff open yure mouth wide
enuff for the noize tew git out without squealing, thro
yure hed bak as tho yu waz going tew be shaved. . . .
etc.*

But compare Eugene Field (1850-1895) not spelling badly because he thinks it funny but because he
wants a transcript of the way his characters' speech
sounded. One of these characters is telling a story:

*It seems that in the spring of '47—the year that Cy
Watson's eldest boy was drownded in West River—
there come along a book agent sellin' volyumes 'nd
tracks f'r the diffusion of knowledge, 'nd havin' got the
recommend of the minister and 'uv the select men, he
done an all-fired big business in our part of the country. His name wuz Lemuel Higgins 'nd he wuz ez
likely a talker ez I ever heerd . . . etc.*

But observe that there is no need for " 'nd" since we
all use it, more or less, and only say *and* out in full
when it fits to do so. Nor is there any need for "wuz,"
as that is practically what we all say, at least half of
the time, in North America. "Was" is only used, I

imagine, in the Court of St. James—and perhaps even there they say "wuz" when by themselves.

But this extract shows the problem as presented to writers of today. What kind of spelling are you to use for the speech of people who don't talk academic English? If you write a story about Noranda miners, or deep-sea fishers, lumberjacks and hi-jackers—How do you make them talk? Not like divinity students, certainly, and even apart from profanity, as discussed in an earlier chapter, something has to be done to convey their peculiar speech and accent. . . . But make it as little as possible. Such a little goes such a long way. Any form of dialect or odd talk spelled out in crooked spelling gets tiresome to a degree—as bad as Esperanto, or simplified spelling or basic English.

The true method is to suggest peculiar talk rather than to do it out in detail . . . a touch here a touch there. . . . See how wonderfully Mr. Montague Glass manages the speech of his *Potash and Perlmutter;* inserting with it here and there such verbal gems as *tchampanyer wine* . . . and such phrases as . . . *That depends on what you call it sick, Abe; I don't got to see no doctor exactly.*

When special accent and dialogue are thus artistically suggested the reader quite unconsciously carries it along all through, quite unaware that the bulk of the language is plain straight English. That's the way to handle your deep-sea fisher, let him say ahoy! and abeam and awash once or twice and he'll run straight the rest of the time.

Thus far we have been mainly concerned with explaining what not to do, what to avoid. Having ruled out puns and bad spelling and play upon words generally as at best mere incidental things in the expression of humour we naturally ask for some guidance in the opposite direction. By what method and in what way can a writer train himself towards the perception and expression of humour? Now humorous literature is of varying grades. Such things as puns and bad spelling are at the very bottom. Above them comes the broad field of burlesque writing, and above that field again a charming ground where humour rises above nonsense to present amusing scenes (not burlesque but actual), amusing episodes (not upside down but right side up), and above that again the presentation of character in the light of humour, and highest of all, the sublime humour that reflects through scene or character the incongruity of life itself.

A word as to each of these indicated divisions.

Burlesque humour is seen in such works as the operatic verse of Gilbert and Sullivan, the pages of *Punch,* the *1066 and All That.*

The humour of character, in its simplest form, gives us some odd or peculiar individual, distinctive and attractive, who then becomes a medium for talking about things in general. Such characters run all the way from the *Sam Slick* of one century ago, past *Mr. Dooley* of half a century ago, to *Charlie McCarthy* (most peculiar of all) on next Sunday's radio.

But on a far higher plane, as no doubt *Charlie McCarthy* and *Mr. Dooley* wouldn't admit, are the great characters which stand of themselves in the world's library of humour, represented by such master-presentations as those of Sir John Falstaff, Monsieur Jourdain le Bourgeois Gentilhomme, The Vicar of Wakefield,

Mr. Pickwick, Tartarin, and Huckleberry Finn. When humour reaches this height it blends laughter and tears so intimately together, in its view of the contrast of life's little yesterday and unknown tomorrow, that it becomes not the lowest but the highest form of literature.

Through this extended range, where can instruction or precept come in? Is there any way of telling anybody how to do it, or of helping instinctive art to better itself? Undoubtedly a lot of things. Read and ponder on good models. Read them not once but again and again. Notice, if you like, where the author falls down—where Dickens begins to cry, and Mark Twain gets prosy. But still more heedfully, note where the writer does not fail—does it just right. Is there any distinctive attribute that we can trace out in this wide field to imitate, any sort of quality that runs all through this gamut, from the bottom rung of burlesque to the top platform of sublimity? This first: All humorous writers—even more so than writers at large—have to learn an extraordinarily nice usage of words. Other writing sometimes gets so exciting, as to what is happening, that it ceases to be dependent on single words and phrases. When good old Edgar Wallace used to get his sleuth hound shut by the villain in a cellar with the water rising and the temperature falling and hope fading—it wasn't a matter of words. The fellow has to *do* something. Such wonderful story tellers as Mrs. Belloc Lowndes can hold their readers (I know of one anyway) enthralled, without doing so by the power of single words or chosen phrases. The single sentences all seem ordinary. With the humorist it is different. If he wants to hold the reader he's got to do it with his words and they must be exactly the right ones.

Let us consider some examples:

Mr. Pickwick meets on a coach a boring fellow-traveller, a Mr. Peter Magnus, who calls his attention to the curious nature of his initials.

*"You will observe—P.M.—post meridian. In hasty notes to intimate acquaintances, I sometimes sign myself 'afternoon.' It amuses my friends very much, Mr. Pickwick."*

*"It is calculated to afford them the highest gratification," said Mr. Pickwick.*

.   .   .   .   .   .   .

One might search the universe for a more apt phrase, for bringing out the contrast between the size of the expression and the triviality of the object.

.   .   .   .   .   .   .

Now here is Mark Twain in that extraordinary make-believe story *Cannibalism in the Cars*. Readers may recall that it arose out of the incident of certain Western congressmen getting snowbound in a train and getting very hungry. Mark Twain builds this up; makes out that they got so hungry that they turned cannibal. But they did everything by legislative procedure, even the choice of their victim.

.   .   .   .   .   .   .

*Mr. Harris was substituted on the first amendment. The balloting then began. On the sixth ballot Mr. Har-*

*ris was elected. . . . There was some talk of demanding a new ballot . . . but the happy announcement that Mr. Harris was ready drove all thought of it to the winds. . . .*

*Next morning we had Morgan of Alabama, one of the finest men I ever sat down to.*

. . . . . . .

Or here is J. M. Barrie in *My Lady Nicotine* in a burlesque sketch about the killing of an editor by a contributor. In the police court evidence is given by a policeman that Mr. So-and-So came hurriedly down the stairs from the editorial rooms and said, "I have killed the editor." The policeman answered, *"Then you ought to be ashamed of yourself."*

. . . . . . .

Look again round the globe for an answer for the policeman and you will hardly beat that.

Nowhere is the need of the "right word," the *mot propre,* more pressing than in the section of humorous writing represented by comic verse. This form, a sub-division of burlesque writing, flourished mightily in the nineteenth century and never dies. One thinks of James Russell Lowell's matchless:

*John P. Robinson he,*
*Says they didn't know everything down in Judee.*

Or of Bret Harte's immortal Heathen Chinee!

> *Ah Sin was his name*
> *And I will not deny,*
> *In regard to the same,*
> *What that name might imply.*

Or one crosses the ocean to hear W. S. Gilbert in
his *Bab Ballads*

> . . . *Strike the concertina's melancholy string,*
> *Blow the loud-voiced harp like anything.*

And so on down to the brilliant and satirical verses
of our day—with Gelett Burgess, Guiterman, G. K.
Chesterton and Hilaire Belloc.

.     .     .     .     .     .     .

Now if you examine comic verse with a view to writing it you will see that the essence of its literary appeal lies in the extraordinary correctness, aptness and
simplicity of its words and phrases. It rhymes in an
effortless way. There must be none of the painful car-
pentering, the poetic license, which shifts accents and
distorts pronunciations to make a stanza fit together.
Compare:

> *The sons of the prophet are warlike and bold*
> *And quite unacquainted with fear. . . .*

So sings the bard of Abdulla Bulbul Ameer, or more
commonly, Abdul the Bulbul Ameer. How neatly and
smoothly the verse runs; and the happy phrase *quite
unacquainted with fear,* instead of "afraid of nothing."
It reminds one of the "highest gratification" of Mr.
Peter Magnus mentioned above.

Or let Captain Harry Graham recite for us his verse
about the Baritone Singer:

> *Will no one tell me why he sings*
> *Such doleful, melancholy lays,*
> *Of withered summers, ruined springs,*
> *Of happy bygone days*

*And kindred topics more or less
Designed to harass or depress?*

The virtue lies in the *more or less designed to harass
or depress* . . . the peculiar prosaic phrase *more or
less,* as if fair-minded measurement was needed; and
the (apparently) quite accidental way in which *more
or less* happens to rhyme with depress.

Anybody can easily test his ability and his inclina-
tion to write comic verse. The starting point is found
in the aspect of some tiresome, or over-affected individual, or in some odd incident.

Thus Captain Harry Graham, let us say, suffered
repeatedly in evening drawing-rooms, from the dreadful after-dinner baritone, with his "low necked collar,"
his "fancy evening vest," and his "bloated hand" that
holds, as he sings, his ballad about "faded flowers,"
and "brave kisses." Anybody can visualize him, or kick
him, but it took Harry Graham to put it into verse.
Or again—the writer of Abdul the Bulbul Ameer (it
dates from the days of the 1870's when Afghans and
Russians filled the diplomatic foreground)—the writer,
I say, presumably got "fed up" with visions of terrific
Russians in fur, of scowling Afghans in sheepskin,
overshadowing peaceful people in business suits. The
thought struck him—"I wish they'd go and choke one
another!" . . . and the joyful afterthought, "Perhaps they will. . . ."

Or say that Bret Harte played a poker game with
one or two of the "boys" and a little Chinaman, just
arrived at the diggings, took a hand in, and, to the
merriment of all present, cleaned out the pot.

Or imagine that James Russell Lowell got sick of hearing all the prosy discussion round election times repeating, "Waal! John P. Robinson, he says"—this and that, forever—and the idea flashed into his mind, "Let's use that back and forward as a sort of see-saw of village argument." . . .

Let me now give an example taken from actuality on which a student may work as an exercise. I take an incident which sent a ripple of fun and column comment across the surface of the American and Canadian Press but, so far as I know, was not turned into verse. A local newspaper (I know the town very well but must not name it) carried an item that read:

*The town council last night adopted a cordial and unanimous expression of appreciation of the services of Mr. James Morris, who is retiring at the age of eighty from the post of town clerk after forty-five years of service. The council also voted to Mr. Morris a pension of five hundred dollars a year for life, but not for more than five years.*

The proviso at the end was only a clumsy reference to the fact that the council had no power to vote more than five years at a time. But the opportunity for the genial fun-makers of the columns was too tempting. They quoted the vote and added such friendly comment as:

*Now this is fine, Jim! Five hundred a year for life. But remember, Jim, fair's fair; don't overdo it—don't push a good thing too hard, etc. etc.*

Good enough fun with no malice in it; and I can certify that the venerable recipient of the pension laughed with the rest.

Now turn it into burlesque verse. You would probably find that your instinct would be to make it into a parody of some already known poem:

> *Grow old along with us, Jim,*
> *But only for five years. . . .*

*You are old, Father Morris, the councillors said,*
*And your hair is exceedingly white,*
*But if in five years you consent to be dead*
*We will vote you a pension to-night.*

and so on.

That's all very well. But parody after all is only a second best, parasitic thing. One observes that none of the celebrated poems quoted above are parodies. I think that in this case the proper line of approach would be to use the contrast between the formal language of council procedure and the warm sentiment of gratitude.

A rather odd example of the value of single words in comic verse is offered by the type called the limerick. This means a five line stanza in the familiar form such as:

> *There was an old man in a tree,*
> *Who was horribly bored by a bee.*
> *When they said, "Does it buzz?"*
> *He replied, "Yes, it does,*
> *He's a regular brute of a bee."*

Now those who reduce limericks to the rule and line of metrical propriety divide them into "pure" and "impure" limericks. An "impure" limerick does not mean what the reader thinks it does. Indeed the one just quoted is an "impure" one, and there is nothing wrong with it. A "pure" limerick follows this model:

> *There was an old man in a tree*
> *Who was horribly bored by a bee.*
> *When they said, "Does it buzz?"*
> *He replied, "Yes, it does,"*
> *That* observant *old man in a tree.*

It will be seen that the last line is a sort of repetition of the first, or perhaps of a later line, with a slight variation. The "point" is supposed to lie in the variation, for example, in an amusing or ridiculous use of a single word like observant. This was the proper form of the limerick with its greatest exponent, Edward Lear, in his *Book of Nonsense* of 1846. Many people recall, indeed many nurseries still retain, Lear's picture-book—people with noses incredibly long, and arms to reach anything desired. But ordinary people, not experts, began to find this repeating line rather flat, even if at times the added epithets were particularly apt and amusing. So the last line was changed to allow of a wider range, in fact to represent the main point of the argument. Every one knows Kipling's limerick:

> *There was an old man of Quebec,*
> *Who was stuck in the snow to his neck.*

*When they said, "Are you friz?"*
*He replied, "Yes, I is." . . .*
*But we don't call this cold in Quebec.*

Now if Lear had taken up the pen he would have reflected for a minute and changed the last line to read:

—*that* truthful *old man of Quebec.*

It is an odd example of literary formality. No doubt the French academy of Richelieu's day would have laid down a "correct" form of the limerick.

# CHAPTER XII

## HOW TO WRITE MORE HUMOUR

*Shakespeare re-shaken — Botanising for rananculus —
Humorous narrative — Misadventure: the eternal
John Gilpin — Mistaken identity: Jones is really
Brown — Stories funny all through or funny at the
end — My short theatrical career — The humour of
reported dialogue — Bob Benchley revisits college —
Humorous characters — You only need to find them:
Dickens was so lucky — Dean Elderberry Foible*

WE may speak further of burlesque writing, for although really only the lower range of humour, it coin-
cides, for many people, and especially for schoolboys
and the young, with humour itself. We may try to
indicate here, for people wish to practice it, how burlesque writing comes into being, and in what direction
they may look for a start. The basis of it is the appre-
hension of the resemblance of two things nominally
quite different, or on a different plane of dignity. The
likeness of one to the other enables one of them to be
set in a new light, and its peculiar defects turned into
incongruity and laughter.

Let us suppose that a law student with a sense of
humour, meaning a quick appreciation of the contrasts
and incongruities, is reading over, wearily enough, the
verbatim reports of a criminal law case. He gets weary
of the everlasting "I object"—"Answer the question

please, 'Yes, or no,'" "Did you or did you not?" and all the peculiar jargon that arises out of the rules of evidence. Suddenly it strikes him that this is very different from the law court in the *Merchant of Venice,* the play he read at college and saw acted only the other night. Portia's eloquent and rounded periods— then all at once it strikes him that it would be funny to write up the trial scene in the *Merchant of Venice* as it would be transacted in a criminal court today. This would be the method:

### SHAKESPEARE RE-SHAKEN

*Law Reports*
*Central Criminal Court. Venice*
*A.D. 1598*
*Shylock vs. Antonio*
*before Doge. J.*

THE COURT (*addressing Portia, of Portia and Bellario, attorneys for the Defense*). Come you from Padua, from Bellario?

PORTIA. From both, my lord.

THE COURT. You can't come from both. Answer the question, please.

PORTIA. I did, my lord.

THE COURT. Answer the question, please, yes or no. Do you come from Padua?

PORTIA. Yes.

THE COURT. I thought we should get to that.

PORTIA. Which is the merchant here and which the Jew?

THE COURT. Antonio and Old Shylock, both stand forth.

PORTIA (*to Antonio*). You stand within his danger, do you not?

ANTONIO. Ay, so he says.

PORTIA. Answer the question please, yes or no. Do you stand within his danger?

ANTONIO. Yes.

PORTIA. Ha! I thought we should get to something. Do you confess the bond?

ANTONIO. I do.

PORTIA. Then must the Jew be merciful?

SHYLOCK. On what compulsion must I? Tell me that?

THE COURT. Silence! Don't speak out of your turn. The Court will strike from the record the words *On what compulsion* . . . to . . . *that*.

PORTIA. The quality of mercy is not strained. It droppeth.

STATE ATTORNEY (*rising*). I object. The quality of mercy is not any part of the case.

THE COURT. The objection is sustained. Strike that out. Go on.

PORTIA. Therefore, Jew, though justice be thy plea—

STATE ATTORNEY. I object. She must address the Court.

THE COURT. The objection is sustained. You must address the Court, please.

PORTIA. This bond is forfeit and lawfully by this the Jew may claim a pound of flesh.

THE COURT (*to Antonio*). What have you to say?

ANTONIO. I am the tainted wether of the flock—

STATE ATTORNEY. I object; there is no evidence before

the Court that he's a tainted wether—

THE COURT. The objection is sustained. Are you a tainted wether? Are you pleading imbecility?

ANTONIO. No.

THE COURT. Ha! I thought we should get to that. Strike out the words "tainted wether." Will you please prepare your bosom for the knife. What have you to say?

ANTONIO. But little. Give me your hand, Bassanio; commend me to your wife; tell her—

STATE ATTORNEY. I object. What he tells Bassanio's wife is not evidence.

THE COURT. Objection sustained. Strike out the words *your wife*. Is there a balance here to weigh the flesh?

SHYLOCK. I have them ready.

THE COURT. Answer the question, please, yes or no. Are there balances here to weigh the flesh?

SHYLOCK. Yes.

THE COURT. Ha! I thought we should get to that. Go ahead.

PORTIA. I beg to enter a demurrer.

THE COURT. On what grounds?

PORTIA. He may take a pound of flesh but not any more or any less . . . Nay, if the scale do turn but in the estimation of a hair, thou diest . . .

THE COURT (*interrupting*). Address the Court please, not the Jew.

PORTIA. . . . not less nor more than just a pound of flesh . . .

GRATIANO (*from the body of the court*). A second Daniel! A Daniel come to judgment! Now, infidel, I have thee on the hip.

THE COURT. Who is that?

STATE ATTORNEY. Gratiano, my lord.

THE COURT. Three days in jail. Go on with the case.

PORTIA. . . . if it be so much as makes it light or heavy in the twentieth part of one poor scruple . . .

STATE ATTORNEY (*rising*). I object. He must not take more than a pound but he may take less if he wishes. Your lordship will recognize this as a familiar principle in the satisfaction of a contract.

THE COURT. The objection is quite correct; there is no doubt of the law. Shylock, will you take less? Will you take half a pound?

SHYLOCK. I am content.

THE COURT. Answer the question please, yes or no, will you take half a pound?

SHYLOCK. Yes.

THE COURT. I thought we should get to that. The Court awards half a pound of flesh. The case is closed.

EVENING NEWSPAPER REPORT: Meat case settled. Court awards half a pound damages.

.    .    .    .    .    .    .

It is evident that with a lead like this we might ring any number of changes on the famous court scene. It might occur to us that it could be matched against one of those sensational trials at the Old Bailey in London, to which the world of fashion flocks. They are written up with some such gushing opening as the following:

*The Central Criminal Court, popularly known as the Old Bailey, never witnessed a more imposing or more fashionable assembly than that which gathered yesterday for the sensational case of Rex vs. Ricks. The court was a scene of brilliant light and colour. The scarlet and ermine robes of the Lord Chief Justice on the bench were matched by the brilliant costumes, the flowing silks and flashing jewels of the leaders of the fashionable world. Among them we noticed the Dowager Lady Neverdeigh, Lady Simp, etc. etc.*

Here then would be a fitting "exercise" in the practice of humour, to write and complete such an account as applied to the Doge's court in Venice. Anyone with a sense of humour and a knowledge of the *Merchant of Venice* can see, or rather, feel the effect that is wanted. The only difficulty is to produce it. That is where the difference comes in as between a trained humorist and an untrained humorist. The person without training can appreciate the thing when done, can even make a try at doing it, but is not likely to do it properly, or do it at all without real work and experience. Give a lead to a practiced humorist and he can do the rest. For example, Mr. A. P. Herbert, in one of his lighter articles, strikes the following glorious idea. A visitor is being shown round a garden and is being bored, as we all have been, by the infernal Latin names of the flowers as used by his pedantic, botanical host. So he goes his host one better, by bursting out into ecstatic terms which certainly seem Latin and sound like gardening but somehow don't seem to fit.

Thus:

*Ha! Is that rananculus! And* I say!—your *scrofula* is wonderful!

Now that is all the lead needed by a fellow humorist (in so far as Mr. A. P. Herbert has any fellows). He would be able to go on with it. So the humble student might sit down pen in hand and make a list of flowers that are not flowers. Let us try:

> *Elephantiasis*—no, that's too obvious.
> *Flox*—no, by Jove, that *is* a flower.
> etc. etc. ........ ......Try it out.

Take this similar case. Harry Graham (of the *Ruthless Rhymes*) made one day the startling discovery that for many of our words half of them is just as significant—as "signif."—as the whole of them. Why say "political economy" when "Pol. Econ." will do? Why write *"Hamlet* by Shakespeare," instead of just *"Ham* by Shakes"? Hence Harry Graham was able with characteristic generosity to give this discovery to the world:

> *I gladly publish to the pop.*
> *A scheme of which I make no myst,*
> *And beg my fellow scribes to cop*
> *This labour-saving syst.*

Give that to any trained humorist and he will spin it on as fast and as far as you like. So can you with practice; so can you not without.

All of this, let us remind ourselves, is only in the field of verbal humour, incongruities of language and not on the higher ground of the humour of character and of life. But dexterity with words, even as words, contributes presently to felicity of expression. Yet we must be warned here to leave aside as an exception the punster, who never gets beyond words, a case of arrested development.

We have spoken of burlesque and comic writing as belonging on lower ground than the humour of sustained narrative dealing with character and life. This is undoubtedly true. But we must remember that even from a lower ground a higher altitude may be reached. Burlesque writing at its best is a fine achievement. Nor need any writer be ashamed of it nor be misled into believing that he wastes his talents in devoting himself to it. If he has the peculiar talent he can find no better life work than that of a "funny" writer. It is probable that such people, more than any other writers, have brought temporary solace to weary humanity, have coaxed laughter out of sorrow and brought to those distressed the respite of forgetfulness. If you are funny, keep funny even if it makes you sad.

.    .    .    .    .    .    .

We pass from burlesque and comic writing to the sustained humour of stories. We are no longer talking of the explosive funny stories discussed above but of those on an extended scale. They differ from burlesque in that they are studies of real life or life that could be real if the writer knows how to make it so. Underlying such stories is a sort of plot turning on some contrivance that makes for incongruity. The most time-worn of all such plots is that of discomfiture, misadventure to people for whom, in a small way and not as grand tragedy, everything goes wrong. Such stories have filtered down from the Middle Ages and stand out in such classic examples as the misadventures of John Gilpin. They have long since worn thin. The present rising generation would rather have stories of supermen than of simps, would sooner read—or see or hear—of the cleverness of a crook or the triumph of a detective than of the blunders of a bashful man. This is really, as one might say, going back to Jack the Giant Killer and so it may be that the rising generation is sinking.

A more popular and lasting basis of a humorous story is the theme of mistaken identity. Mr. Jones is mistaken for Mr. Brown whereupon all things may happen. This is especially the case if the two people confused are really of utterly different categories—if an Egyptologist is mistaken for a plumber or a bishop gets mixed up with a janitor, or a lunatic at large is mistaken for all sorts of people.

Now the writing of such stories of a humorous type is much the same thing, in point of technique, as writing stories of a serious type. They need the same art of narration and power of expression except perhaps that this need is greater. Stories of adventure and danger, if sufficiently exciting, can be pretty crude in the telling; indeed most of them are. But stories that are to amuse must move with a surer foot; danger moves fast over bad ground; humour can't.

But even at that there are certain peculiar points of construction that are interesting to consider. One which occurs and recurs concerns the question of how much should the reader know. To what extent do you keep him in the dark, so that when you let him into the light he gets a bigger dazzle. There was a once famous English writer, now mostly forgotten, called Anthony Trollope, who never cared to put a story together without the reader knowing all about it from the start. If the squire was going to be ruined, or the squire's daughter to run away with the coachman, Trollope whispered it first to the reader and then they had the fun together of watching the squire. Writers of our own day on the other hand are apt to be the other way. They hate to tell the reader anything till the last chapter.

Observe first the way in which this applies to crime stories. Critics and analysts show us that a crime story may be told with a concealment from the reader as to who committed the crime and how, in which case the reader, still mystified, follows step by step the work of the sleuth. The story may also be told with a complete knowledge given to the reader as to who killed who and how—in fact he sees it all done. In this last case the reader sits tight and watches the mystified sleuth. Dr. Austin Freeman (better known as Dr. John Thorndyke) calls these two methods "direct" and "inverted." In a preface to his *Famous Cases of Dr. Thorndyke* he explains how, many years ago, he pondered over the problem of the inverted story. If the reader "was made an actual witness of the crime and furnished with every fact that could possibly be used in its detection, would there be any story left to tell?" Dr. Freeman in his experiments abundantly proves that there is.

. . . . . . .

The same problem arises in connection with humorous stories of the kind that turn on a dénouement or final outcome which contains all the fun. Generally speaking, to give away the dénouement spoils the story; indeed this, as already seen, is one of the elementary blunders of the incompetent story-teller. But cases arise where an advanced knowledge of what is finally to happen enables the reader to enjoy the fun all through, instead of waiting, mystified until the end. Sometimes indeed it is a nice problem in technique, exactly like that of Dr. Freeman, whether to tell the story forward or backward—straight on to the end, or make the end known at the start. Here is an example in the story that was originally told by Sir Henry Lucy, *Punch's* famous contributor, about his genial friend Canon Ainger. I and others have repeated it so often that it must be as widely known as it is widely vouched for. But we are talking of it not as novelty but as technique. Here is the story told front first with the end concealed:

*One evening Canon Ainger arrived at a fashionable London house, and as he laid aside his outer things he said to the maid, "Are they in there?" pointing to the drawing-room. The maid didn't know who he was but as there was a large dinner party, just gone from dinner into the drawing-room, she merely answered, "Yes, sir." "Very good," said the canon, "now please don't announce me." Then he got down on all fours. "Now please help me to pull this bearskin rug over myself . . . that's right—now," continued the canon in a whisper, "push the door a little bit open and I'll crawl in." In he crawled on all fours, barking out "Wow-wow!!" as he came. The rug was over his eyes and he couldn't see that this was not the children's party to which he had been invited.*

Now try it the other way:

*Canon Ainger was very fond of children, loved to romp with them and used to turn up unexpectedly at children's parties crawling in with a floor rug over his shoulders to look like a bear. One evening he arrived at what was the wrong house. What was going on was not a children's party but a dinner party and the host and the guests had just finished dinner and gone into the drawing-room. The canon arrived, all mystery and smiles. "Where are they?" he whispered behind his hand mysteriously to the housemaid. "In there, sir," she answered. "Hush!" he said with his hands on his lips . . . "Don't announce me! I'm a bear." "A what!" said the alarmed maid . . . "A grizzly bear," said the canon and added a growl to it. "Now give me the rug . . . " etc.*

From that last point the story runs as before.

Now this question of the relation of the outcome of a story to the telling of a story is a most important consideration in the field of humour. The contrast as explained in the opening chapter is as between humour that runs to a final climax, or dénouement, and humour that reaches no such point but depends for its appeal on being humorous all through. This climax at the end of a story—the *point* that makes the story—is sometimes called the "nub." It's a stupid term, but let it pass for want of a better. As has been discussed above, in a short and simple funny story nothing more than a "nub" is needed. A man can be "put off at Buffalo" amid roars of laughter from listeners, or readers—who never cracked a smile when he got on the train and went to his bunk.

But for any sustained narrative a "nub" alone won't do. No matter how ingenious the ending, how complete the surprise, it is not fair to ask the reader to wade through uninteresting pages to get to it. In fact he won't wade. He'll sink. This is what is the matter with ever so many humorous narratives—nothing to them till the end. Oddly enough, however, at times a humorous story makes a great hit, in spite of this general principle, on its "nub" alone. This is the case of the most historically famous of all Mark Twain's short stories, *The Jumping Frog of Calaveras County*. It was the publication of this story which introduced him to the East. Yet for many people (I am one) it is hopelessly tiresome. It depends for its humour on the idea that a man called Smiley had a frog that could outjump any other frog; another man challenged Smiley (or his frog, or both of them) and secretly filled Smiley's frog with shot. When the trial jump came Smiley's frog sat immovable, shrugging its shoulders like a Frenchman. Now that's all right as a funny idea, but it can't carry the long introduction hitched on to it. Even if the description of Smiley, as willing to bet on *anything,* is amusing, there's too much of it. Other people may think differently. Mark Twain himself thought very little of the *Jumping Frog* till the world insisted that it was very funny.

It is obvious that the thing most to be desired is to write a story that comes to a final climax or nub at the very end but which is of such a nature that it is more or less "funny" from the start and not wearisome to listen to. I submit as an example a story entitled *My Short Theatrical Career* and I fully admit that I wrote it myself although it does not appear in any of my books. Those who know the difficulties that surround quoting other people's stories—question of copyright, of quoting too much, or too little and so on, of offending friends and alienating enemies—will understand how simple and pleasant it is for a writer to quote from his own. In any case I greatly admire the way this story is written. I call the reader's attention, in case he forgets to do so himself, to the style of it, the peculiar measure of the sentences—nothing too much, nothing too little. This makes it carry a singular air of plain fact, or being entirely true—which it happens to be, syllable for syllable.

## MY SHORT THEATRICAL CAREER

*When I was young I had a great fear of doing anything in public and took care never to try to. But through this there came an incident that was very humiliating and made me want to improve.*

*It was like this. I had saved up money for a trip to England and went over in 1893 on the* Laurentian, *an old-fashioned steamer out of Montreal. There were only nineteen passengers. The rest were cattle.*

*Then one night they got up an impromptu ship's concert in aid of the Sailors' Home. The chairman announced from the platform that everybody would be asked to do something, and so I thought out some funny remarks about sailors.*

*But when it came my turn I forgot to say that the remarks were to be funny. Later on, when I became a humorous lecturer, I found that if you are going to be funny you must always say so. But these people couldn't know.*

*So my talk about sailors, or rather my whisper about sailors, was so agonized that it didn't sound funny. It was just insulting. It collapsed in failure and I can feel the humiliation of it just as keenly now, forty-nine years after, as I did then.*

*So I realized that I must not be again caught unprepared in case I was asked to do something before people. I had in my mind, of course, that there would be a ship's concert coming back.*

*So in London I bought a book of Recitations. I think it was Mrs. Palmer's Recitations: I'll admit I know it was.*

*I selected a poem called Lasca, all about Texas, down by the Rio Grande. It begins:*

> *I want free life, and I want fresh air;*
> *And I sigh for the canter after the cattle.*

*I learned it all through, and I kept saying it over, so as to keep my hold on it. I said it over in Westminster Abbey and in the Tower of London. If any of the people I had letters to, asked me to their houses, I kept repeating in the cab, just in case they asked for a recitation:*

> *I want free life, and I want fresh air.*

*But chiefly, of course, I was thinking of the ship's concert.*

*I took my passage to New York in the* City of Paris. *This was a very grand boat with two hundred saloon passengers and all the luxury of the day. There were many celebrated people, Mrs. Annie Besant the theosophist, and a lot of musical and theatrical stars. At the time they seemed tremendous people to me though now no doubt they would just seem nobody as everybody does to anybody who is seventy-two.*

*I knew there was going to be a ship's concert because that was the first question I asked the bedroom steward. "Oh, yes, sir," he answered, "always, sir, the last night out; for us sailors, sir." So I said, "Thank you" and gave him another fifty cents.*

*Then I went out on deck and said:*

> *I want free life, and I want fresh air;*
> *And I sigh for the canter after the cattle.*

*All the way across I kept running it over. I didn't speak to anyone about the concert but I did say once, perhaps twice, to my one or two humble friends in the smoking room that I knew Lasca very well and could recite it.*

*I had a presentiment that something was going to happen. On the day of the concert a big printed program was posted. But my name wasn't on it nor any Lasca. I felt half glad and half sorry. It is like that when you are all braced for adventure.*

*The concert was very grand with everybody in evening dress. I sat in a corner at the back. Mrs. Besant made a theosophical talk. Then all of a sudden in the middle of the program I heard the chairman saying:*

*"And now, ladies and gentlemen, we come to an item of our entertainment which we have not put upon the program but which I know you will enjoy as a special treat. You are to listen to a recitation of the poem* Lasca. *Those of us who are Americans know it well and love it and those here who are British will, I am sure, share in our admiration. I won't name the gentleman who is to recite* Lasca *to us, but he is in the audience and I'll just ask him to make his way . . ."*

*It had come. I got up from my seat and started to move along the side of the saloon towards the platform. It was, I think, the most tense moment of my life. The chairman was going on with some remarks about* Lasca *but I couldn't hear him. I was repeating over to myself:*

*I want free life, and I want fresh air.*

*Then I noticed that across the saloon on the other side there was a big, ungainly-looking fellow making his way along just as I was. I thought at first he was just changing his seat but then I realized he was trying to get to the platform, and the people were making way to let him pass. Then I saw the people all looking towards him, and whispering, and breaking out into applause.*

*I stood still.*

*The big fellow got to the platform and there was a great burst of applause.*

*"And now, ladies and gentlemen," said the chairman exultingly, "you are going to have the unannounced treat of hearing Mr. De Wolf Hopper recite* Lasca."

*De Wolf Hopper with perfect poise and assurance put out one arm and said in a resonant voice that filled the room:*

> *I want free life, and I want fresh air;*
> *And I sigh for the canter after the cattle.*

*I had sunk down in an aisle seat. No one noticed me. I had got free life, but I wanted fresh air the worst way.*

. . . . . . .

Now the above story is all very well but one has to admit that the weak side of it is that it is altogether a narrative in retrospect, all comment and no dialogue. Many people would think it lower in class than a story which has the same air of being undeniably true and consists largely of actual dialogue, actual conversation. This achievement of humour by reproduction of what seems actual conversation with no comment, no explanation is amazingly good art. When well done it looks so utterly simple as if doing it were nothing.

Certain conversations are funny if you can manage to present them just as they were said. You will think this the easiest thing in the world. It is one of the hardest. Try it. You no sooner put down the words said than you are afraid that the reader won't catch on to it, or won't get it all. So you find yourself putting in guide marks and comments. Instead of writing, "Yes," said Smith, you put down " 'Yes,' said Smith with a look of hopeless perplexity," or "with a sigh of relief," or with something or other that should have been left to the reader to put in.

The practice of the present volume has been to avoid

citing and comparing the writers of the present hour.
But in this case some of them—and notably Robert
Benchley and Dorothy Parker—so greatly excel in
this peculiar art that it seems more reasonable to name
them than to refer back to people, such as preemi-
nently Anthony Hope, who made their mark in it
years and years ago. Here is Mr. Benchley describing
what happens when a college reunion gathers together
the old classes of graduates.

.    .    .    .    .    .    .

A familiar face! In between the bead portières
comes a man, bald and fat, yet with something about
him that strikes an old G chord.

"*Billings!*" *you cry.*

"*Stampfer is the name,*" *he says.* "*Think of seeing
you here!*"

*You try to make believe that you knew that it was
Stampfer all the time and were just saying Billings to
be funny.*

"*It must be fifteen years,*" *you say.*

"*Well, not quite,*" *says Stampfer,* "*I saw you two
years ago in New York.*"

"*Oh, yes, I know that!*" (*Where the hell did you
see him two years ago? The man must be crazy.*) "*But
I mean it must be fifteen years since we were together.*"

"*Fourteen,*" *he corrects.*

"*I guess you're right. Fourteen. Well, how the hell
are you?*"

"*Great! How are you?*"

"*Great! How are you?*"

"*Great! Couldn't be better. Everything going all
right?*"

*"Great! All right with you?"*
*"Great! All right with you?"*
*"You bet."*
*"That's fine. Kind of quiet around here."*
*"That's right! Not much like the old days."*
*"That's right."*
*"Yes, sir! That's right!"*

.　　.　　.　　.　　.　　.　　.

Now what was needed in order to put together that admirable little vignette of actual life? First, the eye to see, the ear to hear, the mind to hold. Many, many people have been at college reunions and have half seen these things, but have seen them as through a coloured glass. A man goes to the reception with the preconceived idea, one altogether kindly and wholesome and well meant—that it's a great thing to see the "boys" again. So it is, only somehow you can't find them. You only see what Mr. Benchley saw. The "boys" seem to fade into a sort of abstraction. You can never locate them till they're dead, and then it's just too late.

And now, observe that it is a condition of such humour that it must be perfectly kindly, no ill-will about it. If anybody set out to show that the bond between a graduate and his old college is a dirty mean business, just cheap selfishness on each side, the college "making strong" out of the graduate and the graduate "making strong" out of the college— Oh, well, a person who sees it that way is looking at it not through glasses rosy with affection but through glasses all split into distorting prisms, showing everything in false perspective. Humour, it cannot be too often said, must be kind.

. . . . . . .

Those who know Miss Dorothy Parker's work will set beside Mr. Benchley's reunion her matchless story of the husband and wife, moving towards estrangement by the sheer banality of their daily intercourse. The topic seen, as a whole, is not humour but tragedy; the humour breaks through in spite of it in the photostatic conversations.

. . . . . . .

Now when we say that these conversations of the stories of the college reunion and of the domestic estrangement are written down *just as they are said,* that is not quite so. They are written down just as they would be said if they were said just as they ought to be said for the purposes of humour. Granted that one seizes the *idea* of the flat, banal question and answer, then art goes a little past reality in seeing to it that the sentences are just a little bit better than real. Oddly enough we do not, as readers, recognize this. We say, "Isn't it exactly the kind of conversation at a reception?" Well, as a matter of fact, it isn't; not exactly; it's better.

. . . . . . .

We have spoken of humour as expressed in the comic play of words. We have spoken of humour as arising out of the "funny" incidents and incongruous scenes. But for the highest ground we must move up to the humour that arises out of human character. Here incident and setting are only contributory. The character is the thing.

By humorous characters we mean people who in their queer individuality and odd actions convey something of those contradictions and incongruities of our lives out of which humour arises.

Now there are odd characters all round us, for those who can see them. As a rule we do not do so till some one points them out. A humorous character must be a person whose essential nature is pleasant to contemplate, with a minimum of malice, so small and ineffective as to be harmless, a minimum of hate, or else a hate so gigantic and so futile as to be laughable. Such a character must, by his own outlook, live in a kindly world. To this may be added some little oddities of speech and gesture, little touches of absent-mindedness, and an odd incapacity for simple things. Such characters as a rule must ripen with age. Dickens, it is true, created the immortal character of the Fat Boy. Funny boys as a rule are very tiresome.

There is a singular misunderstanding about the question of authors' "characters" and where they get them. People seem to think that they need only go round and look for characters as one looks for four-leaf clovers. Once you are lucky enough to find them, all you have to do is to write them down just as you put your four-leaf clover in an album. Thus we are told that Charles Dickens *took* Mr. Pickwick from such and such an old gentleman he used to see out walking, that he *took* Mr. Micawber from his father, Mrs. Nickleby from his mother and Mrs. Gamp from some one or other of the damp old women of his London who drank gin beside corpses. Dickens, you see, was very lucky. He *took* characters in hundreds—

there are, I think, about 1900 people in his books.

Now go and *take* Mr. Pickwick yourself. I'll walk him up and down for you and you *take* him. I'll have him clean his spectacles and wipe his forehead, drink a glass of sherry with you—and then you *take* him, you just put him down on paper if you can. And you can't. More than that you won't even see him; you won't know it's Mr. Pickwick. You'll just think it's a rather ordinary middle-aged man (Dickens thought Pickwick old but he wasn't).

You see, the process of *taking* a literary character from a living person runs exactly the other way; the genius is in seeing the literary character. Dickens didn't take Mrs. Nickleby from his mother; he had the genius to see that his mother was Mrs. Nickleby; in other words he took his mother from Mrs. Nickleby.

. . . . . . .

Now the difficulty with writing stories that rest on a character is that the reader, being only a reader, won't let it go at that. He must have action. He begins to ask, "What happened?" No story can run along on mere description without some kind of a goal post finish. It is this difficulty that prevents many people from writing humorous stories who otherwise could do so. To put it very simply, they could begin them but not end them.

As an example, let us suppose that you have been greatly struck by the laughable yet lovable character of your old college teacher Dean Elderberry Foible. You used to notice in his class his little vanities, his affectations, but instinctively you appreciated his enthusiasm over literature, his gleaming spectacles and glowing countenance as he spoke of Beowulf, or recited a passage from Chaucer. He seemed able to admire anything, things you couldn't touch, all sorts of stuff that you knew to be punk. Indeed you presently felt that he lived in a world of his own, all brightened up with enthusiasm, in which everybody important seemed tremendously important, and in which, therefore, a harmless vanity might take immense satisfaction out of casual compliments, small distinctions—a seat on a platform or a place in a procession.

So you felt that if you could only write down Dean Elderberry Foible on paper you could make a marvellous short story out of him. More than that, you could turn him into a "series," a "character," and let him walk off on his own into the literary world and take you with him.

So I can imagine that you would undertake a beginning something like this:

*I always think of my old teacher Dean Elderberry Foible as one of the most remarkable men I have ever known. The Dean himself would have denied this flatly, and said that anyone must have known hundreds of men more remarkable than himself or, if not a hundred, certainly fifty, or anyway twenty-five. At least this is very like what he once said in the class about classical scholarship when some had asked him whether he ranked as the leading classical scholar in America. The Dean laughed at the idea. He said that there were easily a dozen men his superiors, or at any rate, half a dozen. Indeed he could think off-hand of two. He admitted that they were both dead.*

Somewhere about that point, or after a page or so more of generality, it will occur to you that you must make something *happen* to the Dean. But as far as you remember, nothing ever did happen to him. You couldn't make him commit a murder and you wouldn't want anybody to murder him, and of course he couldn't steal—so he's clean out of line for crime. As for love —sex-appeal at sixty with a bright bald head and glittering spectacles and Chaucer—that's not possible. Nor can you send him to the war, or get him mixed up in politics, or embezzlement. So there you are. Here's the Dean all ready to go into a story and you can't get a story to fit him. Nor is this true of the Dean only. There are all sorts of characters round you that you know you could write down—or you think you could—and yet you can find no story for them.

Now the solution of this problem is that if you can write them down, go on and do so and they will find a story for themselves. You will be surprised how small a point is needed as the end or nub or climax if the character is all right. Or rather, you will find that the small point needed for the end once found can easily be expanded, can be written back through the text and seem to have been a part of the story all the time. . . . You have only to look at high-class literary work of this character to see the end sticking out at the beginning. It wasn't there at the author's start at all. It was shoved through after. The real start, that they first thought out and got into words—is the character.

. . . . . . .

This advice is easier to give than to take. I am myself the person who knew Dean Elderberry Foible and have wanted for thirty years to put him on paper. If I do not succeed soon in doing it, I shall offer him to a crime writer to turn him into a detective.

. . . . . . .

With that I end this book. The main idea in it is that writing originates in thinking. The basis of thinking is sincerity and interest in the world around us. If you can add a kindly good will towards man that is an even firmer base.

Writing can never be achieved by learning what to avoid and what to leave out. There must be something put in before you can leave anything out. Writing comes from having something to say and trying hard to say it.

# INDEX